M000009480

Diamond

in the

DARKNESS

ABUSED CHILD
of DARKNESS,

RECLAIMED DAUGHTER
of LIGHT

PEGGY CORVIN

"Because the God who said, Out of darkness Light will shine, is the One who shined in our hearts to illuminate the knowledge of the glory of God in the face of Jesus Christ. But we have this treasure in earthen vessels that the excellency of the power may be of God and not out of us."

2 Corinthians 4:6-7

Copyright © 2020 by Peggy Corvin.

Diamond in the Darkness: Abused Child of Darkness, Reclaimed Daughter of Light

The information contained in this book is the intellectual property of Peggy Corvin and is governed by copyright laws of the United States and international convention. All rights are reserved. No part of this publication, neither text nor image, may be used for any purpose other than personal use. Reproduction, modification, storage in a retrieval system, or retransmission, in any form or by any means, electronic, mechanical, or otherwise, for reasons other than personal use, except for brief quotations for reviews or articles and promotions are strictly prohibited without prior written permission by the author.

ACKNOWLEDGMENTS:

Cover and Interior Design Services by Melinda Martin—Martin Publishing Services

PUBLISHING INFORMATION:

NLT—Scripture is taken from the New Living Translation, copyright © 1996, 2004, 2007 by Tyndale House Foundation. All rights reserved.

KJV—Scripture is taken from the King James Version. Copyright © 1999 by New York: American Bible Society.

NKJV– Scripture is taken from the New King James Version®. Copyright © 1982 by Thomas Nelson. All rights reserved.

NIV—Scripture quotations marked (NIV) are taken from the Holy Bible, New International Version®, and NIV®. Copyright © 1973, 1978, 1984, 2011 by Biblica, Inc. ™ Used by permission of Zondervan. All rights reserved worldwide. The "NIV" and "New International Version" are trademarks registered in the United States Patent and Trademark Office by Biblica, Inc. ™

ISBN: Paperback 978-1-7348118-7-2

      Hardback   978-1-7348118-8-9

      eBook   978-1-7348118-9-6

PUBLISHED BY: SOUTHWESTERN LEGACY PRESS, LLC

P.O. Box 1231, Gallatin, TN 37066

Email: swlegacypress@gmail.com

Library of Congress Control Number: 2020905600

LIBRARY CATALOGING:

Corvin, Peggy (Peggy Corvin)—Author

Diamond in the Darkness: Abused Child of Darkness, Reclaimed Daughter of Light

145 pages 23cm × 15cm (9in. x 6 in.)

DESCRIPTION:

"Diamond in the Darkness: Abused Child of Darkness, Reclaimed Daughter of Light" tells the author's journey from the darkness of childhood physical and emotional abuse, through an encounter with God, to a life lived with Him. As a tenant farmer's child, Peggy was born into poverty and hunger and abused by men who had power and no heart. Adoption saved her life but landed her in a family dominated by alcoholism and rage. Starved for nurture and love, she finally reached a point of giving up on life itself. An unbidden powerful encounter with God changed everything about her heart, but nothing about her circumstances. Step by step, God's Word and Presence lead her as the profoundly entrenched strongholds are broken, and her life is transformed. This book shows the depth of darkness so readers can come to understand the Power God has to change lives eternally.

CONTENTS

Dedication

STAN CORVIN, THANK YOU! THIS BOOK WOULD NEVER HAVE HAP-pened without your encouragement and the profound love you show me every day. Thank you for your insights, your visions for this work, your knowledge, and your expertise as you wore your editor hat. I am so blessed by you and grateful you see the Light in me. Thank you for your soft whistle during those times I have to find my way back. Thank you for holding my hand as we go through this life journey, standing on the Rock, loving each other, and the Light!

Precious children, Mack, Karen, and Kevin, as I wrote about the dark times, it stirred up even more gratitude for each of you. How blessed I am by the loving, giving adults you became despite all I took you through during your childhood. You dazzle me with the Light you show to the world. Thank you for your lavish, undeserved love and acceptance of me! I love being your momma.

This book is sincerely dedicated to all who have survived physical and emotional abuse as young children when you should have been loved, nurtured, and protected. My prayer is that this book will help you find your way to the One who can take off the darkness from those experiences and show you what a precious, Light-filled being you are!

Jesus, thank you for not giving up on me, for loving me relentlessly, and for your lavish grace and mercy. Thank you for entrusting me with the honor of telling about You through the story of my life.

Peggy Corvin

Introduction

I WAS BORN INTO ABJECT POVERTY. I USE THE WORD ABJECT ON purpose. It wasn't just that we were poor. Make no mistake; we were very poor. Think gray unpainted shotgun shack on the edge of a cotton field in backwoods Louisiana. Dirt road. Dirt yard. No running water. Outhouse. Allowed to live in another man's house as long as we worked the cotton fields. But abject? Well, that means utterly hopeless, miserable, wretched, cast aside. It's the perfect adjective!

It is hard to write this story. Not hard because I have to go back and think about it all and to then bring it back into my world. It is a long-ago part of my story, never forgotten, but no longer painful, no longer defining me.

It is hard to share with you. All I write about is factual—it is the actual story of my life. This early part—the story of the darkness, tells about the things that happened *to me*, but not about who I am. Usually, when I tell this story, I hear responses like, "You poor thing." My heart leaps up, and I respond inside with, *"Are you kidding me? I'm one of the richest women I know!"* I see responses on faces that want to label me—victim, abused, damaged. Those labeling words don't belong on me. I also see sympathy. And in that sympathy, there is no acknowledgment of power. I want to meet your eyes and let you see deep inside me—the real me, so you can see for yourself what powers me. Of course, since you are reading this, that is not possible, so I will try to find the words to let you see into me. That is what makes this hard.

I encourage you to press through this journey with me into the darkness so that you can come to the place of Light. That place where the soul understands redemption, where the amazements are stored, and where, once felt, the power that is life itself pulses. I must write of the darkness so you can understand the power of the Light. And as you stand in that place of awareness, with a knowledge which passes understanding, I pray you will know hope.

SECTION I

The Darkness

In the beginning was the Word, and the Word was with God,
and the Word was God. He was in the beginning with God.
All things were made through Him,
and without Him nothing was made that was made.
In Him was life, and the life was the light of men.
And the light shines in the darkness,
and the darkness did not comprehend it.

JOHN 1:1-5

CHAPTER ONE

Abject Poverty

"GIT IN THE TRUCK, GIRL," THE BIG MAN GROWLED IN MY DIRECtion. My stomach tightened, I sought help with my eyes. My mother looked down and kept emptying her cotton sack into the bin. Her dirty-blonde, wispy, unkempt hair blew across her face; she made no move to clear it out of her vision. As I turned my eyes toward my brother, he met my seeking with cold eyes yelling a warning. With a quick tilt of his head, he showed me what he expected of me. Climbing into the bed of the truck, I settled onto a stack of empty cotton sacks. It felt good to sit down. We went to the fields early in the day; as soon as the wind and sun dried the cotton bolls enough. Even though my sack was a small one, it got heavy as I filled it. Wearing the sack stretched across the front of my body, I walked with the grown-ups for the duration of the day. At five years old, I never questioned it; I knew better than to do that.

The truck bumped down the dirt road at a halting pace. Deep, uneven trenches on either side of the road kept travel slow and resulted in a jolting ride. The Louisiana "gumbo" mud made for unstable road-beds. The rusted pickup turned and climbed up the levee, down the other side, and finally came to rest under a thick stand of hardwood trees beside the slow-moving river of water stained reddish-brown as it cut a path through the dirt of the land. The shrill sound of the cicadas filled the air. Their piercing scream was describing exactly the way I felt inside, and I wasn't sure if I were joining in with them or not. At that moment, I was totally capable of making that sound with them. I wanted to make that sound. But I was silent.

The man was large and dirty, and he was somehow able to reach over, grab me, and pull me from the truck without ever looking at me. This had happened before. I knew what was coming; I felt sick but had no choice. I was alone. He shoved me down and pinned me with one hand. I knew not to fight; when I had tried, it just ended up hurting worse. I had the scars from the burn marks to wear as a reminder. I knew not to scream. I knew not to. But the power of the scream in me was stronger than my ability to contain it. From somewhere deep within me, I joined the cicadas and screamed out my anguish. Enraged by my scream, the loathsome man delivered the slap with such force it shook my teeth and left my ears ringing. The cicadas were silent.

Hopeless to escape, all fight gone, I endured what was happening. Eyes squeezed tightly shut. Hands clenched into tight fists; but not as weapons, I was just trying to hold on to me. Then peace came over me, and I heard, "*Look*." Not from the man did I hear that, but from inside me. I squinted up into the canopy of tree leaves and caught sight of a large beautiful yellow butterfly. Then I looked, really looked.

I watched as it circled above me. Captivated by the movement, I followed the flitting, gliding, regal creature as it made it's way ever closer to me. Shadowy darkness enveloped me; by contrast, the butterfly seemed to be made of light. In my heart, I became the butterfly; all else faded away, and I flew, and glided, and sailed easily, freely.

Finally, the man left. Slowly becoming aware of my surroundings again, I realized I was on my own. I made my way to a log at the edge of the river. After a bit of time, I eased myself into the sun-warmed murky water, not seeking a cleansing as much as some form of comfort. Tiredness settled into every part of my body as I let the water soothe me and help me let go. A few brief moments passed before I began to realize how hungry I was. Slowly coming up out of the water, I began my walk back through the shadows and across the levee, hoping the rest of them had saved me some supper.

I have no memories of laughter during the first years of life. I have no memories of ever being looked at, or at least not of looking into anyone's eyes. I do remember the filth. I remember the hitting. I remember hearing commands said with authority. Mostly by men who always seemed angry with me. There was no yelling. There was no crying—only anger-powered commands and being hit if I didn't comply. As the youngest of eight children living in that sharecropper shack, my role was to stay out of the way and do as I was told. There was rarely enough food and most of what there was went to the men—the stronger workers. Most days, I was pressed into working in the cotton fields. I pulled weeds and made sure I grabbed and killed any worms eating the cotton plant as I did. And I picked the cotton when it was time. Other days I was home alone. Not needed, making sure I didn't bother the others.

On one such day, I climbed up into a cabinet in the kitchen and was helping myself to some food. I remember scooping out a fingertip full of lard from the bucket and then dipping it into the sack of flour to coat the lard. Sucking on my finger until it was all gone, I wiped my finger dry on my dress and repeated the process. My simple dress was made out of the same material as the beige flour sack. Engrossed in the process of eating, I did not realize someone had come up to the house until I heard the door open. Fear shot through every part of me! I quickly pulled myself into the cabinet and held the door as nearly shut as I could, squeezing my eyes together tightly. All I can remember thinking was, *"Oh no, oh no, oh no; this will be awful if they find me."* My ears were buzzing as a roar of fear surged through me. Taking food was not allowed!

I felt the cabinet door being pulled opened. I could not bring myself to open my eyes to look. Caught in a world entirely controlled by dread, holding my breath, time stretched, and became interminable. Thinking I knew what would happen, I braced for the force of the coming blow. I was thrown off when instead, I heard the sweetest sound I had ever heard. "It's okay, it's okay, I'm not going to hurt you." The words, while very contrary to what was usually said to me, weren't what impacted me. It was the sound of the voice speaking them that moved me. I had no frame of reference for this gentle and comforting sound compelling me to find the source. Opening my eyes, I saw a woman standing there. This woman was different than anyone I had ever seen. Her dress was yellow and seemed to float as she moved. I didn't know her, yet she seemed familiar. "It's okay, come on out. Are you Peggy?" Looking down at the mention of my name, I gave a nod. "Oh, I haven't seen you since you were a little baby. I'm your aunt, Sue," she explained. This had no meaning for me since I had never heard of her. She coaxed me out of the cabinet and down off the countertop. As I stood before her, I watched her face as she took it all in. Fresh burn places showed on my elbow, the preferred location for administering punishment. The bruises weren't as evident. The filth covered those pretty well. But she knew, and I knew she knew. I watched her face as it registered disgust, moved through sorrow, and landed on some sort of anger. I waited. Powerless, I possessed a deep resolve just to accept whatever happened next, it never occurred to me to run away. Would she slap me, or turn around and walk away? Neither. Instead, in a moment that has stayed with me forever, she got down on her knees and wrapped me in her arms. Whispering, "I'm sorry, I'm so very sorry," she held me. I didn't understand her words; however, the hug had deep meaning for some never-before-experienced part of me. I had no idea the impact that moment was to have on my life.

Next, she did something else no one had ever done. She asked me a question, "Do you want to come with me?" Not sure what I was to do, I just let the response coming from inside me flow up, go past my brain, and come out of me. I nodded yes. I didn't know where she was going, but I knew I wanted to be with her. After digging around in her purse, she found paper and pen, wrote a note, and then loaded me into her car. We didn't take anything. There was nothing to take.

As we left, she turned down the part of the road that didn't go into the cotton fields. I had never been this way before. I watched for a while as other houses and other people slid by my window. But I wasn't drawn to any of that. I was content in the presence of this woman, the one that was so different. After a little bit of time, she invited me to lay my head in her lap. Resting on that soft bundle of yellow cloth, I fell into a deep sleep.

Later in my life, I came to understand this woman was my mother's sister. She had made it out. Out of the darkness. She refused the label *"poor white trash"* and went in search of a new definition for her life. In the late nineteen forty's and early fifties, women were just beginning to come into the workforce. My aunt left Louisiana, moved to Mississippi, got a factory job, and made her way to a better life. She had not come back to visit until that day. I don't know why that was a day I was home alone, but I'm so grateful it was.

She took me to her home, gently waking me as we parked out front. I had been in such a deep sleep I wasn't sure if this was a dream or not. Huge trees with branches stretching down to the ground offered their big white flowers that filled the air with their scent. There was a burst of color from flowers growing everywhere out front. I wondered if they were like the flowers that grew on cotton. I wondered if they would change their color three times in three days and then die. As we went inside, I felt disoriented. I had never seen anything like it. Up to this moment in my life, everything had been "grime" gray. This house held color and soft textures. I didn't have words to describe this; I just knew it was everything that was not part of where I had been. As she glanced down at the front of her dress now stained the color of me, she gently said, "Let's get you a bath." These words were gently said but intensely carried out. I still remember the nail brush she used that day.

Speaking reassuring words constantly, my aunt set out to separate me from the effects of what had been my life. She pursued and re-moved all the filth. The tub had to be emptied and refilled two more times. The filling of the tub fascinated me; you just turned a handle, and the water came out. As she washed and scrubbed and cleaned, she examined. Several times her eyes filled with tears, but even with a quivering chin, she smiled at me. She looked, really looked at *me*, and her response was a smile. Seeing that, something else from deep within began to lose its hold on me that day. Finally satisfied her task was complete; she opened her suitcase and dressed me in the outfit she had made for me. "I have a friend who has a daughter your age, so I made this to fit her," she explained. It was too big for me, but it was beautiful and clean. I loved it.

My aunt was on the first vacation she had taken from her job. The plan had been to visit family in Louisiana. Instead, she went back and rescued me. In that era, single parents, daycare, and unmarried women raising children were virtually non-existent. I don't know what it took for my aunt to find a new life for me. But I know she was determined I would never go back to where I had been, and she saw to it that I didn't.

Within days I was in a different old farmhouse with a very old couple. My aunt said she was taking me to "My Mama," so she could keep me until I got a new family. Said in my aunt's soft southern voice, I thought she called her "M'mama." They lived in a small little house, and I slept on a pallet on the front screened porch. Since I thought it was her name, I called her M'mama, and she called me young'un. She fed me a lot, mostly vegetables from their garden. I was allowed to play in their yard, but I couldn't chase their chickens. Several days I wished she had told her chickens not to chase me.

A short time after I was left with M'mama, the day came when I was told someone was coming to meet me. It required more scrubbing, this one in the washtub in the kitchen. When I was clean, my hair was put up in bobby pins until it was dry. I was given another dress which had been made for me. This one was made out of flour sack material, but it was blue with little flowers scattered over it. This one fit.

A hard rainstorm had moved through earlier that morning. I was sailing my leaf boats carrying their stick people in the puddles left in the front yard when a big car pulled to a stop at the edge of the road. I ran to the front steps and sat down. It was where M'mama told me to stay, and I tried to pretend I had been there all along. Two men got out of the car and stood there staring at me. My stomach hurt. M'mama came out to the porch, and by way of invitation, called out, "Y'all come on down." Then she admonished me saying, "Stand up, young'un, so's they can see you better." I locked eyes with one of the men. He was very big, but he looked me in the eyes, and in that moment of connection, I experienced calmness. I slowly stood up and smoothed down my dress. As I reached my full height, the clouds parted, the sun warmed the now curly top of my head, and it became a very bright day. The two men stayed for a while, and *"That Tall One"* kept asking me questions I had no answers for, but he seemed nice and made me smile some.

This encounter led to my going to live with my new family within two weeks. My aunt came on a weekend and loaded me into her car; this time, I had a few things to take with me. She was taking me to live in my new house with my new family because, as she explained, she couldn't take care of me since she had to work, and M'mama was just too old. "But," she said, "you are going to be so happy, just you wait and see." The rush had been because school was going to start, and everyone knew I needed to go to school. Everyone, it seemed, except me.

CHAPTER TWO

My New Family

I WAS TAKEN TO MY NEW PARENTS' HOUSE, AND AFTER A SHORT visit, my aunt deposited me with them. I was left there after clinging to my aunt, asking her to, "Please don't leave me. Please take me with you." It was the first time in my life I had ever asked for anything; it was the first time in my life I had something I didn't want to lose. I received a stern admonishment to hush up and behave. Hush up I could do, but how I was to behave here was completely foreign to me.

It was a quiet afternoon in the nicest house I had ever been in, the woman cooked, and "That Tall One" talked to me some and showed me around the house and yard. He was very kind. He showed me a big plant he said was an "elephant ear" because he said it looked just like the ear of an elephant. I remember thinking if I ever did see a green animal big enough to have an ear like that I sure hoped it wouldn't act like the chickens.

After supper, they made me take a bath, but they didn't scrub me. Then they took me to the room they said would be mine and told me to get into the bed where I was to sleep. Other than pallets at my aunt's house and on M'mama's porch, I had never had a bed to myself, much less a room. I climbed into the clean bed that had freshly-ironed sheets; I had no words to express how that felt, but an involuntary smile came across my face. They turned off the light and turned on the attic fan. The fan's rotating blades pulled in the fragrance from the gardenia plant blooming outside my window, filling the room with the best scent I had ever smelled. I had a full belly, my body was clean and cared for, a wonderful bed wrapped me in a sense of safety, and oh, that amazing smell, yet I was so sad, silent tears ran out of the corners of my eyes.

My world was gone; with all the awfulness of it, it was still the only world I understood. In that world, I knew what was expected of me. I knew how to stay out of trouble most of the time. I was one of them. Now knowing my aunt was gone forever, there was no going back. I really wanted one of her hugs. I felt an unbidden flash of anger, wishing she had never hugged me in the first place. *"That won't be a problem here."* I thought. *"Who are these new people? How can I ever be one of them? They are so different."* I felt totally alone, and I was more afraid of what lay ahead of me than of anything I had come through. I don't remember ever having cried before in my entire life, but that night, I quietly made up for it.

Two days later, on Monday, Mother and Daddy went to work. They had coached me to call them that over the weekend. While they were leaving, Elizabeth came. She was a dark woman, like some of the women picking cotton with me. This was so good. I thought, "Maybe there will be more of these kinds of people." And that is the way we began our lives together. They went to work, Elizabeth came and kept me and did all the housework. All I had to do was play; for the next week anyway. Then, the following Tuesday, after Labor Day, I started first grade. In those days, you started school at the end of summer, and there was no kindergarten. I knew nothing of the culture or society of school. I had no readiness skills, no friends, and no sense of family. I don't remember ever having seen a book, let alone having someone read one to me. Somehow I survived, and graduated twelve years later with an advanced High School Diploma and went on to graduate from college. The fact that my undergraduate degree is in education with an "early childhood specialty" probably has its roots in my experience with learning about school.

I was not the run-of-the-mill, normal child. I isolated from the other children. They were all so silly. They played "games"—I had no idea what they were doing, and they laughed at me when I didn't know. Quite frankly, they reminded me of the chickens. My proficiency in being able to stay out of the way and not doing anything to call attention to myself served me well in those first days. After several days of my teacher telling me, "Erase your paper and do it again until you get it right," I learned to listen intently and to get it right the first time. When you erase a lot, it tears holes in your paper. They don't give you a new one.

Along with learning about school, I was also learning about my new family. They had taken me in quickly and had started adoption proceedings immediately. Apparently, it was met with no opposition. How does a person become willing to take in a child who had my background? Who would want an older child rather than an infant, or at least a toddler? Who would willingly take on the issues I brought with me? Of course, it took me years to understand and to come to peace with these questions. As I share this part of my journey with you, please know it is from a heart absolutely filled with gratitude and love for my mother and daddy. They saved my life. They did all they could to help me have a good and productive life. They taught me many important lessons about how to live that life. And they loved me with all the love they had to give to me. My journey to reach this understanding, however, was a long and arduous one.

My daddy was instrumental in arranging the adoption. He met my mother on New Year's Eve in 1941, and they married seventeen days later. It was during the frantic early days of World War II when decisions were often made in haste. After years of marriage, several things had become apparent to him. My mother could not have children. The doctor performed a hysterectomy. Secondly, it was apparent my mother was angry. Not just a little angry. Little things not going her way sent her ranting and raging at anyone standing in her way. I learned not to stand too close since she often threw things to express just how very mad she was. He thought having a child would make her happy. But, since she had a career she enjoyed and did not want to give it up, he knew she needed an older child. Perhaps one who could go to school while she worked would be a good choice. He thought I was the perfect child to make my mother happy. I was not. No child ever is able to complete the broken places in their parents. But I thought it was just me, that "I" was what always made my mother mad no matter what I did. I thought maybe that was why my first family had gotten rid of me. Perhaps I made everyone mad. I committed to trying harder to make them all happy. I'm not sure why, but it seemed my daddy didn't see the third thing. The alcohol!

CHAPTER THREE

New House New School

A FEW MONTHS LATER WE MOVED INTO A NEW HOUSE. WITH THE new house came a new school. This time I started with the ability to fit in with the other children better than I had at my first school. I had a sweet teacher with a big heart for children. She was kind and gentle as she taught and guided me. At the end of first grade, she asked my mother if she could come and take me to the library each week during the summer. She showed me the books she loved, and we read them together. She kept telling me I was a really good reader, which made me want to be even better. She loved books, but her favorite thing was butterflies. She taught me how to draw them. I colored all of mine yellow.

I settled into a routine of walking to school each morning and home each afternoon. Returning, I was greeted and watched over by Elizabeth as she did the household chores. Mothers of children in my class often helped by including me in activities. One had called my mother and asked if she could take me to dance class with her daughter! I can't even begin to explain how it felt for me to dance. The beauty and grace I felt during ballet class, the genuine smile-inducing fun of tap class, even the discipline of barre and adagio practices thrilled me. Dance was one of the best gifts given to me. My friend's mother was a kind and gentle woman who took me to classes for years. She even spray-painted my shoes and dressed me at the recital. Dance gave me more than rhythm and grace. It gave me a sense of ability. I felt power as the strength and ability of my body grew. Dance freed me; as I danced, I knew I could fly.

Another mother led a Girl Scout Brownie troop, and she called and asked if I could come. She picked me up at school and then took me home after the meeting. I still remember the first time I got to help make cookies with her as we earned our cooking merit badge. Not resisting the temptation, I stuck my finger in the whipped butter and sugar; it was way better than my lard and flour snacks from before. All the other girls laughed when I said I had never made cookies before. I went to summer camp with the scouts, and we sang songs on the bus. We sang "I Know How Ugly I Are" during every trip. I always thought it was one my group had made up since it seemed to say how I felt. Girl Scouts helped me feel like I belonged somewhere.

The music teacher at my school called and asked if I could take music lessons. She told my mother I had a beautiful voice and she would like to work with me. My mother said it was ridiculous; she said she had never heard me sing. We never sang at my house.

Mother and Daddy came home at the end of each day. The first thing my mother did was have a "toddy" so she could relax. She always seemed so tired and was usually pretty mad about some occurrence from her day. After the drink, as her "mad" from the day was draining away, she would then find something to be mad at my daddy for, but if she couldn't, she would get mad at me about something. During the first few years, she would just yell at me, saying things like, "You just always…" and then name something about me like "are lazy" if I had forgotten to do something, or "make trouble" if I had left toys out. The list went on and on. I tried to stay outside or in my room. In the power of her wrath, she had great believability with me. She ruled the roost as they say. She had absolute authority in my life, and if that authority said that is what I was, then it must be true. It sure seemed true because I was constantly making her mad. So mad that the yelling, the screaming, the name-calling led to hitting me. By the time I was in fifth grade, I usually needed a beating at least once a week because I was so bad. I remember the worst one I got.

Elizabeth didn't come every day anymore, and it was my job to help with the housework. Each morning, Mother told me what she wanted me to do when I got back from school. One day near the end of school, as the days were getting longer, I came home from school and went straight out to play with my friends. We played softball in the vacant field a few doors down from where I lived. We had talked about it at recess. Everyone would be there that day, teams were already picked, and I was happy about getting to play. The chores were forgotten. I didn't intend not to do them; I just thought I would do them later. The game lasted longer than usual, and I was in the outfield when I saw my daddy's car turn into our driveway. Fear gripping my stomach, I yelled to my friends, "I gotta go! See you tomorrow," and I ran for home as fast as I could. Walking in just after they did,

I sensed the anger. I tried to explain I was just coming home to do the things she had told me to do, to explain I didn't mean to make her mad; I tried, but I got nowhere. She grabbed me, and while yelling about how lazy I was, saying I was just lying to try to get out of trouble, yelling how I would never amount to anything, she whipped me until she finished being mad. But that wasn't the worst beating I ever got: it was just the first time I felt deep inside me that I didn't deserve it.

That night I did my chores, ate a sparse supper since I had been chewing on my hurt all evening and went to bed with a new feeling. I knew enough people now that I didn't think this was the way she should treat me. While this was so much better than what I experienced with the other family, I began to think this was wrong, too, just in a different way. The next day my teacher sent the children out for recess but asked me to stay and talk to her. She wanted to speak to me about the welts and bruises on my arms and legs. Encouraged by her sympathy, and fueled by a new inner cry for justice, for the first time ever, I told. I told her about my mother and how mad she got at me. I told her the story of yesterday. I told her my mother never did like me. I told.

When the telephone rang that evening, I was in the bath. I heard my mother answer and heard her acknowledge my teacher. Maybe, I thought with hope, my teacher can explain to my mother that I am not bad. Maybe she can tell her she doesn't have to be mad at me all the time. But it was not my mother who was to gain a new understanding that night. It was me. As soon as she ended that conversation, she stormed into the bathroom and began to hit me harder than anyone ever had. It became apparent I had only seen glimpses of rage before as I learned that night what rage fully unleashed looked like and how it felt. Hitting me on my body, not on my arms or legs, she screamed at me the worst things I had ever been called; things I didn't fully understand, but those damning words echoed in my head and reverberated in my heart for years. I was banned from playing with the other children after school. I was banned from girl scouts. She didn't ban me from dance since she had already paid for the costumes for the recital, but she said she would decide next year if she would let me go or not, so I had better watch myself. The next morning she told me I was to go to my teacher and tell her I had lied. And she told me in no uncertain terms that if I knew what was good for me, I had better not ever say anything to anyone about her again. With every hurting, battered, broken-hearted part of me, I believed her.

Junior High brought another friend's mom into my life. I had made my first best friend. She was so happy and so much fun. The astonishing thing was she just wanted me to be happy with her. It never occurred to her I wasn't, so naturally, I was always happy when we were together. We talked all the time. I had never been a talker before. We talked so much that when we were in the same class, teachers tried separating us so we wouldn't talk. So then we passed notes. Finding this much more distracting, the teachers would let us sit in the back, and as long as we didn't disturb others, we could whisper. And her mother liked me! She invited me to their house all the time. Sometimes my mother let me go. I made some of my very best memories with this family. Generally, my mother wouldn't let me go on Saturday night. She needed me to be home on Sunday morning to go to church. After all, what would people say if we weren't in church on Sunday morning? We went to a church that had lots of rituals. All the fifth graders became Christians on Palm Sunday when we knelt at the altar, and the preacher put the Holy Water on our head. I couldn't understand how he made it into Holy Water since I had just seen him fill the silver bowl from the water fountain in the hall right before we went in. They didn't teach that in the classes I had attended. They had only talked about how the church was made. It was essential to my mother that we go to church. If I asked to go to my friend's house instead, she would remind me it was our "civic duty" to go to church each Sunday. We had to go to the early service, too. She liked to have a "Bloody Mary" after church to ease her nerves. We had to get dressed up and wear hats and gloves and sit like a lady; I guess that is what hurt her nerves. My friend's family went to church, too. It was a small Missionary Baptist Church not in the part of town where we lived. Her mother would often take me with them to a "prayer meeting" on Sunday nights. I loved getting to go.

When I was in the eighth grade, I went with them on Palm Sunday evening. My friend had sung a "special," "His Eye Is on the Sparrow." Before the church service, her mother showed me the part of the Bible with those same words. She also read how it said not to worry about anything. Brother Charles talked about Jesus a lot that night. He told us about how Jesus came because He loved everybody and had forgiven our sins. And when He was coming into Jerusalem, He looked out over the people and cried because of what He saw. Brother Charles said Jesus still felt that for us today; as He looked out and saw us walking in our lives without Him, He cried. For the first time, I felt like that had something to do with me. Had Jesus ever cried over any of the things I had gone through? I wanted a happy family with an aching so strong it felt physical. Did Jesus cry when he saw my family? I had continuously heard about all the things I had done wrong. Did He really want to forgive me for them?

At the end of the prayer meeting, we sang a song we had sung every Sunday night, "Just As I Am," and Brother Charles said, "If you feel like Jesus is calling you, just come on down front." I knew Jesus was calling me that night, yet it was hard for me to believe He could love me. It took about four verses before I released my grip on the pew in front of me and went down to talk to Brother Charles. I felt a flood of warmth through every part of me as I prayed the prayer with him, and asked Jesus into my heart. My friend and her mother were so happy for me. There was something new inside me now. They said, "You are going to be so happy, just you wait and see." There was a familiar ring to those words.

My mother was incensed that my friend's mother would think I wasn't already a Christian. We went to church every Sunday so everyone would know we were. And, no, she would not allow me to be baptized at that church. I had already been baptized in fifth grade—end of discussion. There came a gradual lessening of time I was allowed to spend with my friend. And with that, a profound lack of the happiness I had begun to have. The further I felt away from other people, the deeper my sense of not being worthy took root. I remember thinking Jesus may be weeping over my life, but He isn't going to do anything about it. I understood that story about the sparrow though and thought. *"Why should I worry about anything? There isn't anything I can do about it. I don't deserve anything any different than this."* These thoughts became a repeating cycle in my mind, gaining intensity and volume until they silenced the scream of the pain in my soul.

As I finished eighth grade, I had to have a series of assessments to see where to place me for high school. A string of standardized aptitude and I.Q. tests had filled my days. I will never forget the day my parents came with me to the meeting with the guidance counselor. Never before or since has news, which by anyone's standard would be considered good news, had such a harsh effect on my life. As we all sat down around this man's desk, his first words to me were, "You should be ashamed of yourself." "*What have I done now?*" I thought. My face turned hot, then paled as I felt the blood drain from my body, and I went numb. He proceeded to explain I had tested among the top three in my grade in I.Q. and placement in all areas of the testing. My grades, while good, did not reflect that level of ability. Thus the shame he pronounced over me. This was fuel for my mother's ire, and she angrily said, "Well, she's very lazy." From that day on, the standards were raised, and anything not meeting them brought a barrage of browbeating and belittling from her.

Entering high school, I was expected to make an "A" in every class. No excuses. I was also given all the household chores. Since Elizabeth had been let go, it was up to me to clean the house, do the laundry and mow the grass from springtime into fall. Any failure or lack of attention to detail would bring down my mother's wrath. I quickly developed a strong work ethic. I learned everything needed to be perfect. I learned that even in the middle of significant achievements, I usually made my mother mad. When I brought home my first straight "A" report card, her comment was, "It's about time! You should have always done this." I tried very hard to avoid her, particularly until she had her first drink of the day and especially after she had her third. During one of her angry rants about a tiny thing, I vividly remember saying, "I need for you to have a drink." I spoke it to her in mid-yelling, and while this was a true statement, it was not well received.

I had mostly learned how to stay out of the way and to stay out of trouble. The beatings had stopped; the emotional attacks continued with a new ferociousness. I didn't invite friends home; I never shared my life or myself with others. I tried to seem normal at school but failed. I still danced; it was there where my heart still soared. I sang at school in the chorus, joining my voice with others in making beautiful sounds, while I stood next to people who rarely acknowledged I existed. Then I got my driver's license, and that radically changed my world.

CHAPTER FOUR

Daddy

THROUGHOUT THIS JOURNEY WITH MY NEW FAMILY, MY DADDY was the only source of any gentleness or compassion in my life. He was genuinely kind. He shared his love of nature with me and taught me to look for beautiful things all around me. I have so many memories of simple things he would show or tell me. He would find four-leaf clovers all the time and, placing one in my hand, fold my fingers over it and tell me to always hold on to good luck. He would find arrowheads and tell me about the people who made them and how they did it. In the middle of driving down the street to take care of an errand, sometimes he would suddenly pull over, grab his camera from behind the car seat, and off we would go to see a unique flower or the way the sunlight was shining through a tree. He treated me like I mattered to him. He had a great sense of humor and made jokes all the time when we were out doing things together.

He was a wealth of pithy sayings, which I stored up deep inside me. "You never know how far a frog will jump until you goose him," he would say to encourage me to try to do something new. "There's nothing to it, it's just like eating lettuce," was used to keep me from being afraid of something he knew wouldn't be too hard for me if I would try. "If there is a good day out there, I'm going to go get me one," was a view into his daily attitude. This man never saw a problem without going immediately to the solution. Using creative genius was the mainstay of his life and career, and it lifted and carried him out of the hopelessness of our difficult home situation. He took me fishing with him, and we rarely filled our bucket with fish, but always filled our memories with the beauty of the lake we were on; from the swaying of the Spanish moss to the lizard running on top of the water, to the iridescent colors of the water lilies. He gave me beautiful things to cherish. He let me help him with projects he was building. Some of my happiest heart memories were made as I held a board or got the hammer for him. We shared coffee early every morning. Before she got up, we began our days together with quiet talks about nothing in particular, but that time meant everything to me. He let me share his life. He never yelled at me. Not once. If I made a mistake, he would just say, "It might have been a better idea to. . ." I knew he was on my side. He was just as abused by her rage as I was. We took turns taking the full brunt of the attack; we shared the blame for her anger. Having him there reassured me things wouldn't get too out of control. He taught me how to fish, and hunt, and ride a bike, and then he taught me how to drive. He took me to get my license. Shortly after that, he left.

My daddy had taken my mother's driver's license away before

I came to live with them. He felt her nerves were too bad for her to drive. When my mother went somewhere, someone else needed to drive her. He took her to work and picked her up each day. Just after I got my driver's license, my daddy accepted a transfer with his company to a town that was about two hundred miles away. My mother said we weren't going with him. She had worked her way up in her career, and she didn't want to leave. Besides, now, I could drive her wherever she needed to go. It was true; I could drive her; that part of this situation I could handle. But the rest I knew I couldn't handle. I couldn't be alone in this. I couldn't! Why was he doing this? Why was he leaving me? What had I done to make him mad? Why didn't he yell at me and hit me as I deserved? Why did he have to keep it a secret and then just leave me? Other people had hurt me, but this brought anguish I had never felt before. This was the first time I experienced betrayal. He was the only person who had ever given me hope. This was the only time I had ever come to expect someone to be there for me. Why did he let me think he was my rock? When the rock you are clinging to moves, your world falls out from beneath you.

When I had calmed down, my thought was simply this, *"All the things she has said about me must be true. If this man, who is good and kind to everyone, wants to leave me, I must truly be unlovable."* I stopped dancing that year.

CHAPTER FIVE

College

FINISHING HIGH SCHOOL A YEAR LATER, I BEGAN COLLEGE AS soon as I possibly could. I took two full-load summer sessions, followed by twenty-one hours my fall semester. During the first summer session, I ran into a girl from my dance school. She was older, but we had been in a couple of the same dance classes. She had always treated me like a little sister and had encouraged me. She was excited to see me and said I had to try out for the dance and drill team. I got caught up in her enthusiasm and went to the tryouts. Surprisingly, I made the team, and it became a bright spot in my life. It was more drills than dancing, but being on the team was my only real connection to what people call college life. It was great fun to be a part of a team, and the long hours of practice and the push for perfection fed something inside me. I had to live at home so I could drive my mother to and from work, but I knew college was the best chance I had to get out.

I didn't see it as an adventure, or a time for fun. It was a lifeline. Some of the girls wanted to get married and talked about it all the time. Some even joked about getting their MRS degree. As I had physically become a woman, the health classes at school had an impact on me. We heard the explanation of how things worked physically. Teenaged girls were encouraged to stay pure, to have something of worth to offer our prospective husband; that is a beautiful encouragement. And it made me realized my options were few. When you are a girl who has been abused by men, you sit in your silence, realizing you have nothing of value to protect and to preserve. You have nothing to offer since you had your value stolen. "Damaged goods" is emblazoned in your mind and on your heart. You stand condemned by other people's choices to live forever imprisoned with the other unclean, unwashed people of the world. You don't expect the same outcomes as the other girls with you in college do.

One of the girls on the team introduced me to a friend of her boyfriend so I could go to some of the fall football dances and rallies. At the end of our first date, he walked me to the door and said, "You are the girl of my dreams; I think I will marry you." My lips gave a flippant answer. Something like, "That's a great line; why don't you save it and use it when you grow up." But my heart gave a completely different response. Could it be I had a different option? Would someone really consider marrying me? Compelled by this unexpected hope, I fell completely and totally under his control. The hope grew to include an end to the chaos and meanness dominating my life. We dated through my freshman year and married as soon as school was over. My mother was livid and remarked, "I knew you wouldn't finish school. I've never thought you would amount to anything." Such was the blessing over my marriage.

The Vietnam War was raging; people I knew were being drafted and sent to fight, many never to return. It had become a very unpopular war leading our country into a mindset I believe was the lowest point in our national patriotism. We turned our disapproval of the war into actions showing disapproval of the brave men who went into unimaginable evil because they were willing to lay down their own lives for freedom. War protestors used their freedom of speech against soldiers who had fought and paid for that freedom with their blood.

Many men looked for ways to keep from being drafted. Some were willing to leave the country, but there was another way. During this era, if you knew the right people on the draft board, having a wife and a child could result in a 3A deferment. My husband had a dream of becoming an attorney. Our first child arrived in the first year of our marriage and brought with him the new draft deferment. This made my husband's dream a reality. I guess I really was the "girl of his dreams" at that point.

I had begun college at seventeen, married at eighteen, and had become a mother at nineteen. I had no idea how to be married, and I certainly had no idea how to parent a child. All I knew was what I didn't want. With my spoken vows of marriage, I had fervently made some other vows in my heart. I vowed I would never get mad at my husband. I would never yell at him. I would never disagree with him. I would always do what he wanted me to do. I would always make him happy, no matter what it took. Along with my vows, I silently married him to my expectations about this happy marriage. He would always be kind to me. He would be my best friend. He would never get mad at me. He would never leave me. I even said to myself with all the believability I could muster, *We are going to be so happy! Just wait and see!"*

CHAPTER SIX

Marriage and Children

I ENTERED INTO MARRIAGE SEARCHING FOR SOMETHING I HAD never had, reaching for it as if by the sheer amount of my desire, I would attain it. How would I ever find something I couldn't describe didn't understand and hadn't experienced? How would I know where to look? How would I know when I had found it? I had chosen a journey of looking for a never-before-seen sun on a dark and cloudy day.

Through the years, I discovered marriage is not a thing to be acquired. It is the growth of two into one, led by mutual sharing of each one's true self. The problem was I had no "me" to share. I had no identity other than what others had said about me. I did as told; I accepted others' assessment of me. I didn't have a single thought about what I wanted. I only had a clearly defined idea of what I didn't want. I had no respect for myself, so I commanded no respect from others. Very surprisingly, the first years of my marriage were, in my voiced opinion, wonderful. I wanted this more than I had ever wanted anything. The absence of yelling, belittling, and sarcasm seemed to be enough for me. I have heard people say denial is a great place to live. It seems as though that was true in my case. I enjoyed being a wife and thrived on home-making. I cooked meals and baked-from-scratch desserts; I kept my house clean and planted flowers. I took care of all the needs of my husband. I ran his errands, packed his gym bag for his workouts, and went to social gatherings with him. I settled into married life without ever truly knowing how to be married.

My most wonder-filled journey began with the birth of my first son. I had no idea how to care for an infant, but I had bought and read Dr. Spock's *"Baby and Child Care."* It became my guide for his day-to-day care, and I was grateful to have it. However, nothing could have prepared me for what would happen within me. I was absolutely captivated by this child. The word miracle took on new proportions in my head. How perfect, how beautiful, how fun it was to have this little person in my life. He was precious and innocent. How utterly terrifying this was for me. My new vows were all linked to one; "I will never let anything bad happen to him; ever!" I awoke at night in the grip of terror; petrified something had happened to him because I had gone to sleep. As was usually the case, with my vow and my hyper-vigilance, I failed to keep the pledge. I was horrified when at six weeks old, I sun-burned him. There had been snow in early spring, which had prevented me from making sure he got his "at least fifteen minutes of sunshine a day so he would get enough vitamin D." When the sun broke through the clouds, I plopped him in his baby seat, placed him on the floor, raised the blinds, and let him bask in the sunshine streaming in the window. Fifteen minutes later, he was bright pink, and I knew I had overreacted as hot tears of shame ran freely down my cheeks. I grew in understanding how to take care of him, but never let go of the strong desire to make sure he never got hurt.

Five years later, I had a beautiful daughter. My nurse at the hospital remarked she must be a first child because of the way I was taking on over that baby. I remember the first time I held her. I honestly could not breathe. Salty tears from the sheer beauty of her, mixed with bitter tears from thinking I would never be able to protect her, ran unchecked down my face. Grateful for her, but wondering if somehow there had been an enormous mistake. I couldn't possibly be trusted to know how to raise a little girl. My heart vowed I would take good care of her. Eighteen months later, I gave birth to my youngest son. This child brought happiness with him from the moment I held him. He was a gentle child who cuddled in my arms and daily flooded my heart with love. Even in the hectic busyness of life, holding him connected something in me to a deep, ancient feeling of love. My family was now complete. A husband and three children! I now had everything I wished for; a family in which I truly belonged was all I had ever wanted. This was the picture of my complete happiness. Now, as long as I could be good to everyone and make them all happy, it would be alright.

Normal, routine, genuine life consumed my days for the next few years as I made a home for us. All the chores of washing, wiping, cleaning, straightening, sewing, cooking, yard work, housework, schoolwork were colored and shaped by the sounds of happy children. I had beautiful children who talked and sang and giggled and shrieked and held my hand. They looked piercingly into my eyes as I tried to answer their deepest questions. Sweet voices whispered their secrets into my ears. Little arms with often sticky hands hugged me so closely and often that I couldn't tell where I ended and they began. My nursery rocking chair was often overfilled with all four of us curled into each other. I stretched my arms around them, holding us tightly together and softly sang, "summertime and the living is easy." Amazed by their unique expression of beauty, I was intrigued by how each personality was different. I was positively dumbfounded that they were birthed from me. The ache I felt inside when I looked at them was another birth pain; pure and undefiled love germinated, took root, and began to live in me.

The role of mom dominated my time, my energy, my heart, and my attention. Perhaps that is why I missed the early signs that my role as wife was changing. Only in retrospect did I realize my husband's workdays had grown longer, required that he had more quietness when he got home with no interruptions from the children, and that an occasional beer had become a daily scotch sought as soon as he walked in the door. Our social lives became agonizing experiences for me. I knew I wasn't pretty or well dressed like the other wives, and he often told me how stupid my friends were, and I understood what he was implying about me. One evening I fueled the fire when at a cocktail party, I was drawn out of my silence by a lively discussion about environmental issues. I shared some recent relevant research data but was unprepared when another person asked where I had gotten that information. My honest response of, "From the "Weekly Reader" brought howls of laughter and my husband's blistering berating later at home. There is no loneliness quite as bleak as the loneliness you feel sleeping eighteen inches away from another person.

A chasm had opened between us; he was going in an upwardly

mobile direction in his world, I was burrowing deep into the safe confines of mine. For two more years, I tried to hold on to order as we lived in a world splitting apart. His alcohol consumption increased drastically and fueled previously dormant anger, which, when left unchecked, gave way to rage. The rage directed at me brought back my dark version of the truth. It had never left; this brief sense of false security just silenced it. When the chasm grew into a bottomless pit, it shrieked its eternal dark truth, "See, you are completely unlovable!"

CHAPTER SEVEN

Divorce

THE PIECES OF MY WORLD FLEW APART AND WERE FLUNG INTO nothingness. They each wore labels which increased the power of their trajectories. Infidelity, rejection, betrayal, fault, divorce, severed bonds, settlement, dissolved forever, single, destitute, alone, broken. As the horrible words and sounds of that world's explosion subsided, a deep and profound silence sifted down and settled over my life taking up residence in my very being. There was nothing I could feel, all thoughts stopped, I couldn't move. I tried to breathe, but there was no air. I somehow existed outside of my body. It was months before I could think. And when I did, my first real thought was, "*What will happen to my children?*

Standing completely alone in life, I remembered my vow never to let anything bad happen to them. That vow jump-started activity in my life again, and I set out to provide for them. I took a teaching job so I could be with them as much as possible, but it never provided more than their very basic needs, and sometimes not even that.

The years that followed were desperate. On top of all the hyper-critical labels given to me by my family, I walked around clothed in the label "divorced woman." Now the world knew I was unlovable. Conveniently, having grounds for divorce gave me a new label, and I chose "victim" as the name I wanted the world to use. Fear gripped me continually and motivated my decisions. Whatever ability allowing me to connect with others I once possessed had been severed by the sharp pieces of my shattered world swirling around me. I made new vows. I would never let any man get close enough to me to make me vulnerable, I would never trust another best friend, I would never, ever again expect to be loved. But even in this cold place conditioned by a heart frozen in fear and pain, I knew I could not raise my children alone.

Wandering around in the barren wasteland of a shattered life, shape-shifting mirages spring up giving the illusion they will satisfy your deepest desire and fulfill the needs you are incapable of meeting. It is like standing in the middle of a blistering hot summer road, looking at the shimmering waves ahead. It seems certain that what you see ahead of you is the clear water needed to quench your driving thirst. You are compelled to run head-long into the mirage. There was a frantic need at the core of me and a multitude of oases springing up with the promise of cool water. I ran after most of them. Over the years which followed, I entered into a variety of relationships which I thought could help me survive. Every relationship was one of reciprocity. It was always one in which I saw there was also something I could provide as long as it didn't require "me." I could provide care, support, and daily tasks, but was unwilling to give myself.

I ran a long way down endless dead-end relationships over the next few years, dragging my children along with me. Desperation-driven bad choices appearing as the source of solution for me ended in devastation and brought ever-increasing darkness into my life. The very ones I sought to provide for and protect bore the brunt of the darkness. Emotionally shut-down, I acknowledged this fact to myself in the usual fashion. I now knew with absolute surety I was indeed a despicable and unlovable person. Even I wanted to leave me.

Alone, kneeling on the carpet, my body completely folded over, forehead on the carpet, I sobbed. The source of this pain baffled me. I was out of money and out of friends. I had once again brought us to this downward spiral terminating in hopelessness. The responsibility of caring for my children overwhelmed me. But I had been here before. This time though, I was utterly exhausted. I had nothing inside at all. As I crumpled to my knees, I sank into the abysmal storehouse of the brokenness of my life. The nothingness inside began to be filled with the long-suppressed pain resting dormant in the depth of my soul. I sobbed until I could kneel no longer, then lay straight out, face-down, and sobbed continually. *"Let me die, let me die, let me die."* was the broken litany I spoke between sobs. Realizing I seemed to be addressing this to someone, a fleeting thought brought God to mind. *"Why did you even let me be born?"* More of an accusation than a question, this articulated agony brought a new wave of pain. *"If you are God, tell me why I am so unlovable that even You don't love me. Tell me so I can just die and be done. I can't live like this anymore! God, help me!* With that imploring declaration, the dam forming the strong fortitude holding me up broke; emotion poured out of me and filled the room with tangible darkness. My demanded request of God hung unanswered in the air waiting while I was finally completely broken, all hope extinguished. Darkness enveloped me and completed its victory over my life.

SECTION II

The Light

"Do not gloat over me, my enemy! Though I have fallen, I will rise.
Though I sit in darkness, the LORD will be my light."

MICAH 7:8

"Where can I go from Your Spirit?
Or where can I flee from Your presence?
If I ascend to heaven, You are there;
If I make my bed in hell, behold, You are there.
If I take the wings of the dawn, If I dwell in the remotest part of the sea,
Even there Your hand will lead me,
And Your right hand will lay hold of me.
If I say, "Surely the darkness will overwhelm me,
And the light around me will be night,"
Even the darkness is not dark to You,
And the night is as bright as the day.

PSALM 139:7-12

CHAPTER EIGHT

The Encounter

FACE-DOWN, LIFELESSLY PRONE, I WAS SUSPENDED IN A TIMELESS place devoid of sound or movement. Almost imperceptibly, a mild current moved through me. I couldn't tell if it were a breeze or electricity. Becoming aware of it, I sensed a presence with me in this new realm. Quick, fleeting glimpses of an ethereal *"Something"* occurred and continued as the current became stronger. Then I saw the yellow butterfly take shape, become defined, and rapidly begin to move directly toward me from its great height. My body began to respond, resuming my kneeling position I raised my head. In its swift motion toward me, the beauty of this celestial being exploded just before my eyes. I physically felt the impact as an explosion of intense opalescent light filled my surroundings. Tangible rays of light entered every shadowy place invading the depths of me. I was immediately warmed as my pulse raced while my breath was suspended. This light illumined everything in my life.

From my vantage point, I knew I was at the bottom of a dark pit oozing muck all around me. As I watched, a mighty, open hand gently scooped me up and settled me securely in the hollow of its palm. The swirling light began to reveal the activity behind each shadowy bit of muck as I was being lifted up. In this timeless place, there was no hurry motivating the hand as scene after dark scene moved from the story of my life into sharp focus as the light directed this upward journey. No dark deed escaped the light's scrutiny. Even the most horrible acts that perpetually extracted a high price for me to keep them hidden lost their power as the muck was stripped away with illumination. Still silent, I stored up insight from each vivid scene in my role as an observer.

This journey, which began in the long-ago moved me along until it brought me back to my current situation. Rather than stopping, it then moved further up and beyond. The muck cleared as I was carried higher. The energy inside me grew in volume and intensity as the light began to dominate my surroundings. I experienced visions of unnamable new beings and conditions that exceeded my ability to express verbally. What I saw were the answers for the indefinable longing, the aching pull to something more, and the deep primeval desire living in the very heart of me. I could see the answer up ahead as anticipation surged within me. Then the pace of the journey slowed and came to a gentle stop. The hand carefully placed me on top of an immense boulder and then moved away from me. Standing within the light, I heard words that entered into my being without coming through my ears, and yet they seemed audible. *"I heard you. I love you; I love you, eternally. I have brought you up from out of the muck and the mire of the darkness. You will be safe here where I have placed you. I will always be with you. I will never let you go back into the mire. I will keep the darkness away from you."*

The voice was powerful, captivating, and the most beautiful sound I had ever heard. I breathed in a profoundly filling breath. The energy increased as I began to hear other words spoken in languages I did not understand, yet they conveyed meaning within the deepest part of me. The more I breathed in the light-filled air, the clearer and stronger the words became as they swelled to become a rhythmic sound, and my heartbeat matched the cadence. Every part of my body trembled and quivered with awareness. My mouth began to speak with no input from me and uttered the words I heard. I began to laugh and weep with profound joy. There in the light, I came to life.

Time had no meaning there on the rock where I remained for eons or perhaps mere minutes. The atmosphere surrounding me gradually moved inside me. Becoming aware of my room again, I noticed it had the same furniture, the carpet was still beneath me, but it was not the same. The darkness that had oppressed me in that room was gone.

"Thank you, God." was the beginning of the praises coming out of my heart. I could not stop smiling. The weight of all I had carried through my life was off of me. At that moment, I truly believed I could have flown. Reflection after beautiful reflection of my time with God moved into my thoughts and stored up in my heart. There was so much to take in; there was excitement about coming into the future He has shown me.

After a sweet time of readjustment, I sought to understand how to function in my world after experiencing the ethereal. When I began to think about the practical aspects of my life, I would take a deep breath, which instantly brought peace. My statement, "God, I don't know what to do next," received an immediate response in two parts. *"Never leave my rock; let me lead you to your next steps."*

I floated through the next several days. I didn't know exactly what, but I knew everything in my life was changed. I knew I was not the same person. I knew there was hope; I knew life really was going to be good now. My life circumstances were exactly the same, but I was no longer concerned. I had met God, and He told me He loved me! Each day held a new expectation that He would come back, revisit me, and show me what to do now. The intensity of the illumining light I had experienced was wonderful, and I wanted more of it. As the days progressed, I realized there were new kinds of thoughts coming to me, and there was a definite deep awareness in me I had never experienced. I began to focus on those things and gradually realized they came from that "in me but not of me" place where I had experienced God. After this new awareness and understanding had taken hold, I had a dream. It occurred for three nights.

I was back on the boulder surrounded by light. This rock was a unique substance. It glistened with sparks of light flashing from crystal veins running through it. From atop the promontory, I looked out into the world but could see only darkness. Staying in the pool of light, I ran from side to side and saw only darkness surrounding this area. Then finally, on one edge, I noticed another piece of this same unique rock. As I tentatively put my foot on that piece, it became illumined. Stepping forward, I could see it led to another, then another forming a pathway. As I walked upward on the path, the light was with me. At times I saw other stepping stones not made of the same rock, and if

I stepped toward them, the light would not be with me. As the dream concluded, I could see people made of light ahead of me on the path, and I yearned to be with them. Then I awoke. The third morning I got out of bed with a compelling intent to find those people.

CHAPTER NINE

The Reveal

FROM MY SAFE PERCH IN THE FARTHEST REACHES OF THE BALCO-
ny, I contemplated the demeanor of the white-haired preacher as he
began to speak. My desire to connect with God's people had led me to
consider the only logical place, a church. I found the largest one in my
small Louisiana town. The big white cross placed atop the steeple on
this traditional red-brick and columned church building called to me.
Powerful lights illuminated it at night, converting it to a beacon that
could be seen for miles. This morning, we sang songs declaring our
closeness with God and of fellowship with each other. Then we greeted
each other with smiles which, though broad, never quite reached our
veiled eyes before we settled ourselves to listen.

The pastor announced Isaiah 40 as the Scripture for the morning
lesson. I began scrambling to find it in the Bible I found on the back
of the pew in front of me. I was unable to find it before he asked us

to stand, "For the reading of the Word." I cradled the book in my arms and held it about mid-chest using furtive side-glances to see if my book looked to be open about the same as everyone else's. I could feel my face turning red. Finally, he finished reading, and we sat down. What began next was a beautiful explanation of the greatness of God. It was the first time I engaged my entire being in a sermon. The God this man obviously knew intimately held and measured every bit of our world in His hand. I flashed back to my memory of being cradled in that hand. Bit by bit, he explained how much God cared about every part of the world, and he led us to see He cared the most about each person He had made. The pastor assured us that this same God gives strength to the weak. And in a demonstration of how to use this strength, he showed me what to do next. Moving down from the pulpit to illustrate, he created an image that took root as it imprinted in my mind and stored in my heart; his movements would help guide my choices for years. He used the word repent. "Simply turn from walking the way you are right now," was emphasized as he walked across the platform, then with a clap of his hands he turned and walked in the opposite direction, and "Turn to the ways of Jesus," he said with strength of voice and action. He said it with firmness from a loving passion, which stirred up hope in me. As he finished his beautiful message, I took an offering envelope from the pew back and hurriedly scrawled "*Isaiah 40, Repent, What are the ways of Jesus?*" then stuffed it in my purse. I knew I had gone forward to the altar before, so I was sure he didn't mean me as he called people to the front. Besides, I didn't want all these people to know I didn't know the ways of Jesus. I resolved to buy a Bible and to come and watch them so I could do what they did.

I began my church experience with the mentality of a "pound puppy." I knew I wasn't like these other "people of light." There was too much in my past disqualifying me from becoming a real part of their seemingly perfect lives. Everyone else in my life had pushed me away and kicked me to the curb of life, so I was just grateful God had allowed me into His church at all. And, like a "pound puppy," I wanted to do all I could so I would never be put back out on the curb. Over time, I learned to mirror what I saw in that big church. I brought my new black, Holy Bible with me and learned how to tuck it in the crook of my left arm, thus freeing my right hand to be able to extend a fellowship greeting to those I met. Since my Bible had tabs for all those hard to find books, I made sure to turn the spine outward, so the tabs weren't evident. Each time I came, I heard the call to serve where there was a need. I signed up for everything I could. I brought my children, and we were there every Sunday morning, Sunday night, Monday night to visit the lost, and Wednesday nights, especially Wednesday because they fed us supper, which helped me manage my meager budget. Each week we were also reminded of the importance of reading "The Word." Each weekend I began to gain an understanding of the Bible as I attended Sunday school before the main service.

Based on this new knowledge about the parts of the Bible, I made a decision. I was not here to become Jewish, besides, my deep-south culture and upbringing colored my mindset about Jews; therefore, I wasn't interested in reading the Old Testament since it didn't apply to me. As my Sunday school teacher talked about the teachings of the Apostle Paul, I processed his instructions about women's roles in the church through the filters I had about men. Thus, since I was not interested in being a "Paulinian," I didn't need to read those books he wrote. Left mostly with the four gospel writers' accounts of Jesus, I knew I wanted to be a follower of His ways, so I read those. As I began to have my *"prescribed by the church"* daily quiet time and reading, I started in Matthew. Just a few chapters in, I came to a sermon Jesus had given. I was stunned. Really? He gave a sermon, and someone wrote it down! Why haven't people been talking about that, telling me about that? This, I believed, was undoubtedly the place for me to learn the ways of Jesus. I spent the next year studying the Book of Matthew, primarily focusing on His sermon. It was hard to understand, it was harder to learn to apply it as I came to understand, yet it became my lifeline to Him. I still spent hours at church every week and volunteered tirelessly. I would do whatever was needed, from serving at church fellowships, in the nursery, at vacation bible school to going on Monday nights to witness to the "lost" walking them down the "Roman Road," highlighted in my Bible. I signed up for whatever was needed. I even taught hand bells to third graders one fall, and I can't read music! But the time I spent reading and studying and praying over Matthew's writing was what sustained my closeness with Him. It also led to the next step on the pathway.

CHAPTER TEN

God's Perfect Word

COMPLETELY IMMERSED IN THE SCRIPTURE, WITH NO CONCOR-
dance, with no discussions about what I was reading was neither the
easiest nor the best way to come to understand His ways. I had once,
and only once, asked the deacon teaching my Sunday school class a
question about Scripture. In a moment that silenced the room and
reddened my face, I had said, "But, doesn't this Scripture teach. .
." and in giving my interpretation, I contradicted what he had just
said. He looked at me with a stern warning in his eyes but spoke with
sympathy in his tone as he patted me on my forearm admonishing me,
"Now, Sister, you need to stop questioning, and take it on faith that it
is the way I teach it to you." The topic was speaking in tongues, which
he said had been only for the first-century church. He wasn't open
to hearing my thoughts about his referenced Scripture and absolutely
not my experience with it. So, my quest was solitary as I struggled

through King James verbiage. I was studying Scriptural teachings, which were in opposition to everything the world said was the right way. Thankfully, New King James versions became accepted, so with a new Bible I started back through Matthew. That version was so much better and brought me a new awareness of the meaning of His words. But it also landed me at a crossroads on the path.

Studying Matthew 24, I was engaged in the occurrence of Jesus telling about the events leading up to the end times. He turns to those around Him and says, "Assuredly, I say to you, this generation will by no means pass away till all these things take place." I froze in place. My life depended on Jesus. I knew I had been born in His presence. I felt His Spirit in me all the time. I heard from Him. He was perfect. He knew everything. I finally had a pathway for my life. He couldn't possibly make a mistake! He just couldn't! And yet, those things haven't happened yet, and that generation is long gone. My thoughts were frantic. If He was wrong about this, what else was wrong in these teachings? The agony and dread that comes only from facing certain death rose from the pit of my stomach and filled me. I sank to the floor and began to pray. Kneeling with the Bible placed on my knees, I began to rock back and forth. My repeated cry to Him, "I need you, God! You have to help me with this", reached crescendo then finally quieted. I found the strength to raise my voice and demand an answer from Him. Accentuating every word, I called out to Him, "Can I believe this book? Is everything in here true?" For emphasis, I struck the book with the palm of my hand. It slid off my knees, hit the floor at the top of its spine, and lay open on the floor before me. A profound hush followed my loud outburst. Then I heard Him command, "Read!" I read:

I waited patiently for the Lord; And He inclined to me, And heard my cry.

He also brought me up out of a horrible pit, Out of the miry clay, And set my feet upon a rock, And established my steps. He has put a new song in my mouth— Praise to our God; Many will see it and fear, And will trust in the Lord.

These never-before-heard-let-alone-read words from Psalm 40 perfectly described my encounter with Him! I had never heard them before, never knew they were in the Bible. He had saved this Scripture just for me; just for this moment. If these ancient words perfectly describing an amazing moment I shared with Him could intersect me at this imperfect place of my wavering and questioning faith, they must be Spiritually created and carried forth. That day, I wept and laughed and praised Him with renewed sincerity of heart as I stood there on the solid stone step of this path He illumined for me. I would never again question the Word of God. I know it is True. I often question my understanding of it and pray, asking Spirit for clarity. And I seek wisdom from other believers of the Word to help glean what He wants me to have. I always test other people's teaching from pulpits and platforms and living rooms and coffee shops against the written Word of God. And with the revelation from this Psalm, I began to seek understanding from other books of the Old Testament and the rest of the New Testament. That day the whole Bible opened up for me as Holy Spirit spoke: "Read." He issues that invitation to me every day, and I joyfully accept.

I did not resolve my question about Matthew 24 that day. In fact, it would be years before I felt confident I understood what He meant by His words recorded there. I've learned some things will remain a mystery until we get to Heaven. Sometimes I'm just simply not at the place to be ready to understand. I have learned to look to Him to find what He wants to say to me today through His written word. It is always fresh manna.

Removing any doubts about the truth of His Word has created an expectation of encountering God as I study it. My journey has substantiated the truth behind Hebrews 4:12, *"For the word of God is living and powerful, and sharper than any two-edged sword, piercing even to the division of soul and spirit, and of joints and marrow, and is a discerner of the thoughts and intents of the heart."*

The Scriptures are alive and show us what is in our souls (mind, emotions, and will) that doesn't align with Spirit. I lived for thirty-three years without any input from God. During that time, my mind, my emotions, and my will stored up the world's ideas, pain, and unspoken vows based on my worldly experiences. As I study His Word, it changes my thoughts, aligning them with His instead of with the world's ideas. It heals the sadness, the shame, the sorrow stored in my emotions. The hope I find in His Word brings me the joy He promised to give. Understanding His ways and the results they bring strengthens my will, aligning it with His will. And many times, when I have thought my intentions were good, His Word has shown me my understanding of good is not always aligned with God.

Studying Scripture is my place of high worship of Him, where He shows me great and unsearchable things which delight me, give me hope, and of course, lead me to the next level of understanding Him.

CHAPTER ELEVEN

The Parable of the Carafe

I WAS BUSILY ATTENDING TO THE TASK AT HAND. TOMORROW WAS trash day, and I was going through the refrigerator. Each container of leftovers was yanked out and checked for contents that were past their prime. Each shelf was getting a good scrubbing. My body was involved in each motion required of me as I gave more energy to this cleaning than was actually needed. My mind, however, was not involved in this task at all. It was busy ranting at God.

I was mad, and I was telling Him about it. These years of walking with Him had given me a constant awareness of His presence in my life. I loved reading and memorizing the Bible. Things had begun to look so much better in my life. I moved my family to Texas and was able to earn more than before. I taught school for several years but had eventually started my own business. Sales had been a good fit for me since I was highly motivated to close the deals. I was comfortable in my new church and had grown in my ability to serve. I admired the pastor very much. He and his wife were so gentle and giving, and week after week, he inspired me with a powerful message helping me do better things in my life. I learned how to express the new understanding and express how much the Bible meant to me. Yes, things were looking a lot better in my life. And yet just this week, there was another big chaotic crisis in my family. I would say there was a different crisis, but really it was just the same crisis dressed up in a different set of circumstances showing up and bringing pain, confusion, fear, and dread. That's why I was mad.

"Here it is again." my rant continued. *"Why can't I get past this?"* *"After all, I am doing my part! Reading my Bible, witnessing, serving Your Kingdom; where are You?"* I started reminding Him of the promises I had found in His Word. From a very shallow understanding, I lifted parts of Scripture up out of their context and spoke them aloud using a tone conveying my absolute entitlement. Honestly, I kind of yelled at Him and said, *"All I've ever asked You for was a happy family. Is that too much for You to do?"* My cleaning task was keeping pace with the growth of my voiced anger. From the refrigerator, I took out a full carafe of now old tomato juice left from last week's brunch. I was irritated no one had touched it. I set it in the sink and turned the hot water on full force—pouring right into the top of the bottle. While it was being washed out, I turned and finished wiping down the refrigerator and firmly shut the door. Going back to the sink, I was stunned. I had expected the carafe to be cleaned out; however, not one drop of the old, dark tomato juice was gone. Even though the faucet was on full force and aimed into the very top, there was no clean water in the carafe. I turned the water off in stunned silence. Finally, since I was

now quiet, He spoke. *"That is how you are with me,"* He said. *"You are so filled with the things of your past; there is no way for me to come in. You are cleaning the outside, but you are not letting me come in and clean the inside."* Down inside me, I knew He was right.

I had stepped through the doors of the church, found my identity there, and slammed shut the door to my past. All the pain was closed up within me. All the secrets of the dark deeds from my past had been hushed, and I did not want to speak of them again. But like a splinter embedded in my heart, they had festered and still poisoned parts of my life. And just as I would do with a splinter, I had gotten used to it being there except when, occasionally, I bumped up against something triggering the sudden sharp heart pain which couldn't be denied.

The frame of reference informing me of what my new life was to be was an image of the experiences of Disney princesses mixed with a Scriptural view of how Jesus would bring it all into my life. As I followed the ways of Jesus, just as my first instruction had directed, wouldn't He then cause bluebirds to sing around my head and flowers to spring forth on the path of my life as beautiful butterflies settled on each newly formed blossom? Wouldn't I surely walk around happy as could be, and my world would be at peace? Where was my happily ever after?

"Remember where you were when I found you?" His whispered words brought an ache in the center of me. Hot tears quickly followed, but I pushed them back down inside. *"In the dark, miry bottom of a pit,"* I whispered back. *"Remember, I know."* The day I met Him, I knew He knew, He had revealed it all to me. Wasn't that enough? With everything within me, I resisted the idea of thinking, feeling, or even looking at all that again. *"You are clinging to pieces of that past.*

Will you give them to Me?"

I stood still there at the sink. I was rooted to the floor, unable to move, and yet wanting to be anywhere but there. I could hear the soft rhythmic click, click, click of the wall clock as seconds went by. Finally, my sad, but totally honest answer was given. *"I don't know. If I take a step back down into all that, I think I will never be able to get back up. If I begin to feel what I've never let myself feel, it will overwhelm me. If I let myself cry again, I'm afraid I will never stop."*

He didn't respond. After a bit, I took out the trash, wiped down the countertops, and loaded the emptied containers into the dishwasher, except for the carafe. I scrubbed it by hand with water so hot it hurt. I dried it and set it on the shelf.

SECTION III

The Path

I will bring the blind by a way they did not know;
I will lead them in paths they have not known.
I will make darkness light before them,
And crooked places straight.
These things I will do for them,
And not forsake them.

ISAIAH 42:16

But we all, with unveiled face,
beholding as in a mirror the glory of the Lord,
are being transformed into the same image from glory to glory,
just as by the Spirit of the Lord.

2 CORINTHIANS 3:18

CHAPTER TWELVE

Transformation

IN THE FOLLOWING WEEKS, LIFE CONTINUED WITH NO OUTWARD sign of change. The chaos of the current situation was worked out, yet leaving no resolution in my heart. I took care of all my responsibilities at work, at home, and church. I cared for my children's needs, I read the Bible daily as dutifully as I could, and I waited. Was He done with me? Was I done with Him? Had the journey with Him thus far just been imagined by me? Am I really just insane?

More weeks went by. I was getting ready to attend a social function for my work. I definitely did not want to go to it. *"I am awkward and never fit in in these situations; it is so hard for me to go."* I thought. I said aloud to the empty room, "I'm just too ugly to go." Then an unbidden response came. *"There."* He said," *That's the kind of thing I am asking you to give me."* Flippantly I pushed back. *"Give it to You or not, facts are facts, and the fact is every woman coming there tonight will be beautiful, and I am ugly."* Standing on the spoken reality of today, I flung back, *"Okay, so show me how that is something from the past I am clutching!"* Point made. End of discussion. I finished dressing, walked out, and went to the party. Throughout the evening, several women made comments about my looks. Randomly I heard phrases like, "You look so pretty, your face just glows, etc." Of course, I returned each with a greater compliment for them. Inside I thought how odd social mores are; when we have nothing deep to say to each other, we make up compliments.

The following Sunday, I climbed the steps leading up to the large sanctuary. All was well in the sameness of this scene. Flanking each door were men in their dark suits, white shirts, and ties distributing the paper bulletins we needed to guide our worship. Frankly, I don't know if they were the same men each week or not. I usually never made eye contact, just took the bulletin, and said, "Thank you." This morning, however, the man by the door on my path said, "You are such a beautiful woman." In response, I looked at him with eyes stunned wide open but had no words to speak. He immediately turned the brightest red I have ever seen a person become. By way of an apology, he began to stammer, "I have never said anything like that to a woman other than my wife. I have no idea why that came out of my mouth." He seemed as shocked as I was. He was an older gentleman, so I assumed he had just gotten me mixed up with someone else. I smiled and let him know I wasn't offended. I went inside and sat on my customary pew in my usual place.

CHAPTER THIRTEEN

The Mirror

THURSDAY MORNING STARTED EARLY FOR ME. I HAD FINALLY gotten an appointment with the buyer in a large company, so I didn't want to be late. *"I need to beat the rush hour traffic into Dallas."* I thought. Several suits, which were actually the same suit, just in different colors and textures hung in my closet. Each Sunday afternoon, I organized them in the order I would wear them in the coming week. I hung blouses, etc. alongside each, so there was no scramble, no choosing, and no chaos. It didn't matter which one I wore since I would look the same no matter what. I put on the suit of the day and then finished my hair and make-up, giving attention to each individual part without ever really looking at the whole. Eyelashes were given another coat of mascara, some of the blush got another layer of powder, and flyaway strands of hair were sprayed into submission. *"Well, that's as good as this is going to get,"* I thought as I turned out the light and left the room. My commute was stressful, but as I drove, I reviewed in my mind the types of wire this customer needed. They were a major fire alarm company requiring expensive cable wire. I knew I had samples in my case and thought through the structure of each. I finally arrived at the tall, gleaming office building which housed my customer's business on one of its floors and parked in the adjoining garage. The lobby was busy, causing me to wait at the reception counter before I could sign in and get approval to go upstairs.

I was nervous. Looking around the large foyer, I saw many well-dressed, professional-looking women exuding confidence. *"What in the world am I doing coming here?"* I thought. I didn't fit in at all. I didn't look the part. As I rode up in the elevator, I worried that when the buyer laid eyes on me, he wouldn't even listen to what I had to say. But I needed this sale; I had worked hard to get the appointment, so I pressed on. The doors to the elevator opened and as I turned to go down the hall, I noticed a woman across from me. She was a nice-looking woman, and I thought, *"Lord, why can't I look like her?"* With my social face intact, I smiled a greeting toward her just as she did the same toward me. In that split second, recognition set in. *"That is me!"* I thought incredulously. No self-image held within me matched what I now understood was my image reflected in a mirrored wall. Unprepared to come before a mirror, my guard, my filters, and my understanding were off duty, allowing a new image to come into focus. I was utterly shaken by this. I heard, *"You are safe. I'm right here."* I wanted to cry, but I knew my appointment was crucial. I stopped by the restroom, ran cold water on my wrists, took deep breaths until the trembling went away, then pulling myself up to my full height, I continued to my appointment.

Since I had a well-rehearsed sales presentation, I continued in the "auto-pilot" mode. The appointment went so well I left with my first order from the company. That was unprecedented in the industry, but the buyer needed to meet a quota to do business with a small disadvantaged company. I identified with the fact that as a "woman-owned" enterprise, I was indeed disadvantaged. Returning home, I took the rest of the day off. There was no other person I wanted to talk to, nor any other business I wanted to attend to which pressed as urgently on me as my encounter with the mirror.

I sought Him and Him alone. He was not hard to find. In solitude and deep prayer, I simply answered His question I had set aside and said, "Yes, I will. I'm ready to give You all that is in me; all the present, the past, and whatever is in the future." I had been broken and shattered before Him; I had come to Him daily asking for His help, I had read His words asking Him for understanding as I did, I had thanked Him often for the wonder of Him and all He created. I had come to Him crying out for His touch in others' lives. Today for the first time, I came to Him in total submission. Today was the day the broken part of my soul began to mend. Today, who I really am broke through to the place of who I had tried to create in my desperate attempt to rise above who I thought I was. For the first time I longed to give Him all of me; the spiritual me He had given birth to, the physical me still wearing the mire from the past, and the very soul of me with all its denied feelings and entrenched thoughts as I yielded my will and stopped all my trying.

CHAPTER FOURTEEN

Identity

MANY ADOPTED CHILDREN STRUGGLE WITH THEIR IDENTITY. Since I was not adopted when I was an infant, I accepted the identity of those first years and never really actively questioned who I was. The actions, both before and after the change of family, spoke loudly to me!

It was the first thing He addressed that day. He asked me to see myself as a child. I saw a dirty, bruised, scarred little girl. Then He began to show me how He saw me as a child. Many images came. He brought to mind things which had happened and then He showed me where He had been. Though I had no conscious memory of some of these, He showed me experiences which had been bright moments in my life. The first time I had watermelon, the way I loved the smell of cotton as I breathed deeply pressing my nose into the cotton sack, and other small happy things. As these memories were revealed, I knew they were moments I had lived, and I knew He had been a part of them. He also had me revisit the dark things. He took me back to when I was in a crib, a flash of visceral pain seared within as I remembered hands and the pain they wielded, and He showed me He had sent a diversion and kept me alive.

In a sudden download, His Word came into my mind and my heart: *For I know the thoughts that I think toward you, says the Lord, thoughts of peace and not of evil, to give you a future and a hope. Then you will call upon Me and go and pray to Me, and I will listen to you. And you will seek Me and find Me, when you search for Me with all your heart.*

He said, *"You have been seeking Me, but there are places in your heart where you have stored the darkness. You will find all of you only when you let me clean your heart of the mire so you can find all of Me."*

He led me to write out all the labels, names, and descriptions I believed about myself. I took a pad of paper and using a pencil; I began to write. Soon I had a long list and kept them all in a single column down the margin. Oddly, that was the end of my time with Him that day. But in the coming days, if I called myself something, like stupid, for example, I would hear, *"Is that on the list?"* and I added each additional one. He was teaching me to listen to what I came to call my "belief-speak." I knew the Bible, and in my guarded religious façade, I usually measured my words. But what comes out of the mouth in tired, unplanned responses, when one's guard is down, shows what we truly believe.

Early one morning, He prompted me to look at the list. In sessions that came to stretch over days of morning times, He had me remember when I had come to believe each particular thing. He had me write out who had called me that, or how, or why, I came to believe that. Then He showed me how He had seen it. Over time, I finished the list. I came to refer to it as my Master List because it became the beginning point for true transformation as He guided me.

God could have healed all my hurts, all my life in one Holy instant. But as I have come to know Him, I am aware He is a God of process. He could have spoken "Universe," and everything would have been created in one swift movement from this powerful creative God of ours. But He didn't. Genesis tells of the day by day process of forming and establishing our beautiful world. He brought everything into being through an orderly, ongoing, perfect progression. The journey I took with Him has revealed things about His nature and His character that I might never have known without going through this process.

There were many Scriptures addressing this issue of identity, and as I worked through the list, He was so good to give me deeper understanding through them. One particularly surprising revelation for me came from Psalm 139:

For You formed my inward parts;
You covered me in my mother's womb.
I will praise You, for I am fearfully and wonderfully made;
Marvelous are Your works, And that my soul knows very well.
My frame was not hidden from You,
When I was made in secret,
And skillfully wrought in the lowest parts of the earth.
Your eyes saw my substance, being yet unformed.
And in Your book they all were written,
The days fashioned for me,
When as yet there were none of them.

During my pregnancies, I read and studied volumes of books to understand nourishment and how to take care of a child. It was serious business for me. I focused on making sure I got all the nutrients I needed and making sure their diet was healthy. My studies of early childhood development in college emphasized the importance of nurture, particularly during those early years, and of intellectual stimulation. I was diligent and focused on providing everything my children needed. I realized that when I was an infant and young child, I had not had any of that.

Understanding the circumstances of my birth had caused me to place "poor white trash" on my list. It was obvious where the poor came from—we had nothing. But trash came from how they discounted me as an object to be used and then in the end just threw me away. The morning I read this Psalm, He highlighted, *"Your eyes saw my substance, being yet unformed."* He had protected and provided for me in my very formation. With no prenatal care, no nutrition, and no nurture during those early years, there was no natural explanation for the intelligence and the capabilities He gave me. I remembered back to the I.Q. testing for high school and knew He created that intelligence in me. He did fearfully and wonderfully create me there in the lowest parts of the earth. And from the yellow butterfly, and all the other ways he had protected me, even to prompting my aunt to come at just the right moment, He interacted in my days. He had me erase "poor white trash" and using ink this time to write in "Wonderfully Handmade by Him."

The work was far from finished. Every item on the list was addressed over a long span of time. Every lie was erased, and by revelation found in Scripture, replaced by who He said I was. The list was not addressed linearly, but as He brought situations to the forefront. The procedure was orderly and simple to work through. The actual application in my life was harder for me. The lies screamed so loudly in my soul; they often drowned out the truth. I began memorizing Scriptures related to identity. It still took practice, but thankfully He helped me. When I blurted out a negative label over myself, I heard, *"Who formed you?"* other times I heard, *"Whose child are you talking about?"* In those still soft questions, I received His gentle correction. Each time I slipped back, I made amends, asked for His forgiveness, and always found His grace to start over. Because I was buried in darkness for so long, negative self-recrimination was a slippery slope for me. I remembered the dream about the path He had for me. Each time I started down the wrong path, the darkness closed in. It was a reminder to look for the light as I choose my words because they directed my steps.

In another prayer time as I was praying Ephesians 3 over my children, the verse which says, "…that Christ may live in your heart." I stopped and pondered, *"Have I made my heart a good home for Jesus?"* Matthew 12 came to mind. *"When an unclean spirit goes out of a man, he goes through dry places, seeking rest, and finds none. Then he says, 'I will return to my house from which I came.' And when he comes, he finds it empty, swept, and put in order. Then he goes and takes with him seven other spirits more wicked than himself, and they enter and dwell there, and the last state of that man is worse than the first."* That encounter increased my desire to press into cleaning out any miry residue in my heart, but then to be sure to redecorate the walls of my heart with each part of His Word I honestly believed.

Much of my healing came from memorizing what I call "heart

words." They are words from Scripture I truly, deeply believe in my heart, because I knew I would not live by those I didn't fully believe. It's a bit like flying in an airplane. I can read about the way planes work, understand the process of flying, come to see planes are safe, but it is only when I am willing to get aboard a flight and ride into the highest skies that air travel can have an impact in my life. Heart words are ones guiding my choices and actions; I stake my life on them no matter what.

This journey with Him was never an outward striving to achieve holiness. Each step down this path began in submission, letting go, and trusting this was His work He started, and He would complete. Each step, when taken, left me more humbled than before. How could this be? How could this amazing Creator come and spend time with me? It is simply pure, relentless love wrapped in grace and mercy brought to every one of us who will accept Him.

CHAPTER FIFTEEN

Courage

LIKE MANY PEOPLE WHO HAVE GONE THROUGH ABUSE AND TRAU-matic events, I don't breathe normally. This sounds like one of the old "blonde jokes," but I had to learn to breathe. When I was in sales, I took some classes training sales agents on how to get into rapport with their clients quickly. Matching their breathing pace was one of the exercises the group was given. We were paired with other students to practice. After a few minutes, my partner exclaimed, "Will you please breathe?" Apparently, she was about to pass out from lack of oxygen, but this was just normal for me. Living in states of high tension, the expectation of impending doom and repeated trauma leads to holding your breath. Fear was the root of most of my tension. I had a long list of fears. Fear of failing, fear of rejection, fear of people finding out who I really was, fear of hurting my children, fear of not having enough to give them, fear of not being enough, fear of being alone, fear of making people mad. The list caused me to fear living as me. My counselor taught me to box-breathe. Picture using your finger to "air draw" a box as you breathe. Breathe out as you draw the top and first side; breathe in as you draw the bottom and other side. This also became the way I visualized letting out all the rest of the mire as I breathed out, and then brought in Spirit as I breathed in. It was a great exercise to help me get a breath in me, but it didn't restore life in me.

Gently over time, each individual fear was addressed. One morning I was studying Proverbs and read, "The fear of man is a snare." I could read no further. That seemed contrary to what I believed; my mind began a defense against the statement I had just read. *"You better be afraid of man, they will hurt and reject you at every turn; what could God have meant by this?"* My argument continued to build, citing examples of hurtful events, rejections, etc. not just from males, but my concept expanded to mean *mankind*. Fear of them all seemed rational, and in fact, seemed necessary. In my conversation with God that day and for several more to come, I enlisted His support and set out to prove why this one statement in the Word was one that needed adjustment. "After all," I pointed out, "God, You were the first one hurt and rejected by man. Remember, there in the garden, you gave them everything they could ever want or need, and they basically ignored what you asked of them? Remember how you loved them and loved spending time with them, and then they pushed you aside and hid from you? And Jesus, even your very best friends on Earth hurt and rejected You. They betrayed You; they denied being your friends; they never once stepped forward and tried to help you during the hardest part of your journey."

There was so much resistance in me; I knew this must be a deep issue I had. When I finally exhausted my argument, He asked me a simple question. *"How does your fear help you? What does it provide for you?"* A simple question asked was met with easy answers, which did a deep work in my soul. *"It keeps people at a distance. It keeps me safe from them. I always expect to be hurt or rejected, so I'm always prepared for it."*

He let me sit in the utter silence which followed my answers for several days. Then He asked His next question. *"What word describes how you feel?"* "Lonely" was my sad, softly-spoken word. No matter how many people surrounded me, worked along with me, or lived with me, deep loneliness permeated my soul. *"If you will put all your trust in Me, I can change that for you."* His work on this began as I went back to Proverbs and read the rest of that line of Scripture. *"Fear of man will prove to be a snare, but whoever trusts in the Lord is kept safe."* He began to show me that when I trust Him and believe He will be there, He will help me deal with any hurt that comes my way. It is only when I completely trust Him that I am free to love people. This journey of healing took a direction I didn't anticipate as He showed me He would always understand because He had experienced all the things I had.

As a result of what He showed me, the spiritual discipline of communion, known as the Lord's Supper, became a powerful element of my faith. One Sunday morning during church service His words, *"Do this in remembrance of Me,"* grabbed my full attention. I never got past them to listen to the message that morning. He asked me, *What do you remember?* My response was simply *"Just You, Jesus."* The classic image of Him on the cross sprang into my mind. He began to prompt me to look closely at the events leading up to His crucifixion and the details of His resurrection. He wanted me to see something about my life, so I dug in to find what it was. When I reread the story, I understood. His close friend betrayed Him and placed a monetary value on His life equal to that of a slave. His family publicly called Him crazy and rejected what He was doing. He asked for help from friends who said they would be there for Him, and then fell asleep. His closest follower denied ever knowing Him. He was beaten. He was disrespected, and people spat on Him. He was made fun of and jeered. He was stripped naked and physically abused. The list goes on when I considered all He had suffered at the hands of others. It made me understand just what it means to have Him as our Savior. *"You know, don't You?"* I whispered, *"You truly know the pain of life."* I sat on my pew that morning reading about the sin exchanged for forgiveness because of His pain on the cross as fresh tears fell from my heart. Every hurtful, painful, sin-driven act was placed on Him. It stirred me to know everything that has ever been done by me; He took to the cross. Every awful thing done to me; He took to the cross. It takes the mire off me when I realize He took it on Him.

Then from John's writing, I found an even more profound revelation. Throughout the time of the crucifixion, the guards offered Jesus bitter wine. He declined the wine every time until the very end. When He knew that all the sin was there, He asked for the wine. *"I thirst,"* were words of completion. The bitter wine symbolizes the deep bitterness we experience when we hold in the anger and pain from our hurts, letting them fester in our souls. When He took the wine, He let us know He took the bitterness that went with the sin so we could be free of that too. My tears flowed as this revelation filled me. My "fear" of man was founded in a deep root of bitterness over what had been done to me. When Jesus came to earth, He knew people would hurt Him, but He loved them anyway, and He didn't condemn them. I had condemned people, and that kept me from loving and being loved the way He intended for us all to be.

He didn't come to get anything from people. He is God. He didn't need to complete Himself through people; He came solely to love people and to bring the way for their salvation. To follow the ways of Jesus means to have relationships based on lovingly giving to others. This part of my journey has given me a true love for people. Even when someone is acting out in painful ways, I have a love in my heart for them. In fact, I am more passionate about loving those hard to love people because I know they probably have the greatest need for someone to love them—just like I had. Loving people doesn't mean you have to like or support their actions or let them hurt you intentionally. Healthy boundaries are good for me and good for them. Sometimes Holy Spirit prompts me to say to another person that what they are doing is not okay. I am truly making a statement that I believe they are more than their actions. I believe in the desire for goodness, which is innate inside of them. I wouldn't mention their error if I didn't believe they could do things differently. Solomon's words written in Ecclesiastes 3 revealed God put eternity in the hearts of people. Those words help me look past the outer actions and believe in what is in their heart.

Closely tied to this fear was the fear of disapproval from people. The "pound puppy" that would sometimes come back as a soul identity wanted approval. There were times when I craved it so I would fit in, and life would be easy. But there was never a time when obtaining approval gave me peace, or comfort, or joy. My life taught me that approval was tenuous and fleeting, and still, it was a deeply embedded drive within my soul. I had to become intentional about healing this fear. Intentionality was accomplished with two guiding questions I learned from Him: *"Who am I?"* A child of God. *"What does He want me to do in this situation?"* I have never asked that question and not received a ready, clear response from Him. Jesus also began to illuminate the ultimate fear paralyzing me.

As I read Scripture, the miracles He performed while He walked the earth astonished me. The times in which He lived came to life for me. In my heart and mind, the people in the Bible and the situation of their lives were vivid and real. The fear the woman caught in adultery must have felt as she faced the stones caused my breath to catch. Her silent scream, *"What about the man?"* which she could only whimper, screamed loudly in my soul. The shame she must have felt as they dragged her out into public brought an ache to my heart. The incredulous joy that undoubtedly filled her as Jesus looked deep into her and said He had no accusations brought tears of joy to my own eyes. His nature is powerfully loving, undistracted by situations, and focused on the rescue of people, particularly those on the fringes, the shunned, the ones labeled and cast aside. There is no other as powerful as He is; there is no greater love than His. He is the only hope.

But the root of all my fear came sharply into focus as I studied the story of Lazarus. It became abundantly clear that Jesus loved Lazarus, who, along with his sisters, Martha and Mary, had followed Jesus fervently. This family was fully committed to Him. Martha had been a strong, hard-working woman, serving Jesus and the other followers. I felt her frustration at being the one who did all the work as the story in Luke ten relates. Mary adoringly loved Him; she sat at His feet, not wanting to miss a thing He had to say to her. Imagine that. Sitting there with Him, hearing the words, but also seeing His eyes, feeling the impact of His inflection and moved by the expression of His words. What a glorious experience it would have been. Jesus told Martha that Mary had chosen the "better part," and it would never be taken away from her. I felt the soaring power of His words in her heart.

Imagine all the miracles Mary must have observed as she followed Him. She watched and learned, believing more fully in Jesus with every encounter. Truly her faith had become sight as she saw wonder after wonder. In the story of Lazarus' death found in John 11, I came to understand her fear. Her fear brought me face to face with my own.

> *Then, when Mary came where Jesus was, and saw Him, she fell down at His feet, saying to Him, "Lord, if You had been here, my brother would not have died." Therefore, when Jesus saw her weeping, and the Jews who came with her weeping, He groaned in the spirit and was troubled.*

Earlier in the chapter, Jesus said He was going to Bethany to wake Lazarus from his sleep. There is no doubt Jesus knew Lazarus would be raised; this event would produce a miracle so many people would come to believe in Him. He wasn't surprised Lazarus was dead. So, what was it that caused the groaning in the spirit; what was it that troubled Him?

> *"And He said, "Where have you laid him?"*
> *They said to Him, "Lord, come and see."*
> *Jesus wept.*
> *Then the Jews said, "See how He loved him!" And some of*

them said, "Could not this Man, who opened the eyes of the blind, also have kept this man from dying?"

Like the believers around her, Mary believed He could. She stated that fact to Jesus. She completely believed in Jesus' ability. Jesus wept because He understood what Mary and the others felt. Mary believed, in fact, she knew Jesus *could*, but now, neither she nor her friends had faith He *would* do this miracle for her brother.

How many times have I caused my Savior to weep? I look at situations, at conditions, at seemingly hopeless scenes around me and even while walking in my strong belief in Him, knowing He is the one who can bring the answer because I have seen Him do it, I still lack faith He will do that for me.

The root of any fear, in fact of all my fears, lies in my inability to receive the relentless love He has for me. Not my "look good" me; my real me. The one who is still being cleaned up, transformed, and still in the process of being returned to who He made me to be. *"There is no fear in love; but perfect love casts out fear, because fear involves torment."* The beloved disciple and apostle John tells us this in a letter intended to carry forth to generations the message that our joy can be made full. Our fears dissipate, our torment ceases, our joy returns *only* when we *know* we are loved; lavishly, abundantly, relentlessly, eternally loved by the source of all love.

As life's tribulations come, I know I have a choice. Do I walk in my belief that Jesus can, or do I walk in my faith that Jesus loves me and will? Faith is the way of Light.

CHAPTER SIXTEEN

Prayer

As He led me through this part of my journey, He taught me about prayer. I also had a maternal grandmother who was a strong woman of faith in a family that gave her continued grief and pain. I didn't hear the term "prayer warrior" until years later, but she exemplified the term. She never experienced any great material wealth. Her husband battled alcohol his entire life and was ultimately injured and disabled because of it. My mother and my grandmother's three other children dealt with addictions, and there were frequent angry outbursts during every family gathering. But through it all, my grandmother had peace, read her Bible daily, and never stopped praying for any of us. I know she prayed for my salvation.

Her youngest son had disappeared and lived his life as a homeless street person. My grandmother never stopped trusting that God would return him to her one day. Anytime she spoke to a friend or family member, she would always ask, "Are you still praying for John? I am standing on God's promise that says, *"Train up a child in the way he should go: and when he is old, he will not depart from it.""* For years she believed, asked people to pray with her, and watched for him to return to her. No one knew where he was or if he was even alive. Her health became fragile as she aged, and my mother and my aunt were trying to decide where she should live, leaning toward placing her in a senior facility. She was heartbroken and begged them to let her stay in her small house. The week before they had to decide, my uncle John arrived at my grandmother's house. He was clean and sober; he had memorized the Bible and came home at the perfect time to be a companion to my grandmother as she lived out her life in her own house. Her fervent prayers had been answered. Her faith was a witness to many and an inspiration to me.

Scriptures throughout the Bible teach us to ask and to ask believingly. The writings from James gave me a sharp warning and reminder as I studied it. First comes the invitation to ask, *"You do not have because you do not ask."* But that is quickly followed by, *"You ask and do not receive, because you ask amiss, that you may spend it on your pleasures."* As I pray, I must align with God's will. That's clear throughout Scripture and highlighted in the Lord's Prayer, *"Your will be done in earth as it is in heaven."* Paralyzing fear sets in when I know that what I am asking is for good. If I am asking for good in a situation and it doesn't come, doesn't that mean He *could do it*, but that He just isn't doing it for *me?*

Pressing in, following Mary's example, I sat with Him in deep fellowship until I finally got the courage to ask Him, *"God, I have seen you answer so many prayers, and yet sometimes, particularly in big situations, You don't answer. Why don't you answer all my prayers for good solutions?"*

In sweet communion, with gentleness, with mercy, and with perfect clarity, He softly spoke to me and revealed the following understanding through a vision. I saw myself coming into His presence, as I walked toward Him, I held out my hands, offering something to Him. He took what I offered, and as He received it, He loved it and treasured it. *"That is the prayer you brought to Me. Each one you bring Me shows you love Me and are bringing your life to Me. I answer every one of them. But I answer them in different ways. Sometimes I say, "Yes, Daughter, that is a perfect way for you right now, and it is my greatest joy to be able to bless you by saying Yes in this situation." Sometimes when you bring things to Me, my answer to you is, "Yes, Daughter, this will be a perfect thing for you. However, you are not ready for this right now. Come here, be with Me, stay near and let me grow you into being ready to receive this." And sometimes when you bring something to Me, my answer is "No, Precious Child, this is not what I want for you. You see, I have something so much better. Draw into Me, stay in the Presence of My Spirit, so that you won't miss what it is that I have for you."*

Profound understanding settled into my Spirit and filled my soul. *"I will never forsake you"* were the words of His which filled me. There are times when I don't understand as I am walking through things personally and with others. Yet, there are times when I look back and can see His answer came in one of the ways He gave me that day.

Thinking about Mary, I know when Lazarus died, she believed Jesus had said no to the message she had sent to Him. He simply did not come in time, or at least in what she thought was "in time." She asked for a good thing. It would be a good thing for Jesus to have kept Lazarus from dying. But, oh, what a fantastic God-thing it was when Jesus raised Him from the dead. He had a much greater purpose for that dire situation. This miracle caused many to believe in His power over death. This miracle reaches out across the ages. Today I hear, *"I can, and I will work miracles which convert disbelief and bring hope where there was no hope,"* resounding from the heart of our Risen Savior. His words grow my faith and restore my hope.

CHAPTER SEVENTEEN

Reconciliation

THEREFORE, FROM NOW ON, WE REGARD NO ONE ACCORDING TO THE FLESH. Even though we have known Christ according to the flesh, yet now we know Him thus no longer. Therefore, if anyone is in Christ, he is a new creation; old things have passed away; behold, all things have become new. Now all things are of God, who has reconciled us to Himself through Jesus Christ, and has given us the ministry of reconciliation, that is, that God was in Christ reconciling the world to Himself, not imputing their trespasses to them, and has committed to us the word of reconciliation.
—2 Corinthians 5:16–19

This is a soul-stirring and sometimes aggravating Scripture when you have difficult people in your life. As soon as I read this Scripture one morning, she flashed into my mind. I had moved three hundred miles away. There had been years of having no contact with her, during which I had pressed into reading the Bible. I had also gone to a Christian counselor, who then recommended I seek help from Al-Anon and Adult Children of Alcoholics groups. Through the guidance of my counselor, whose last name, Love, was a perfect name for her, and also some women who sponsored me, I came to understand different ways to deal with the effects of alcoholism. Because of some of my own unresolved fear of my mother, I chose the Al-Anon slogan "detach with love." Avoidance of conflict had become one of the "superpowers," which took years for me to overcome. It was easy for me to detach since I no longer saw her. It was easy to say I love her, and I am praying for her every day. I know my lips were saying what I thought Jesus would want me to say, but my heart was far from His in this.

Mother Wounds

Trying to "minister reconciliation" with my mother produced an image in my mind of me trying to hug a porcupine. Every time I had come close to her, I always had hope that this time would be different. Every time it ended with me feeling the pain from her barbs. Most of the time, I left thinking that I had made her day since I had given her a reason to get mad. Frankly, I was no longer willing to be the reason anymore. There was a long list of why I couldn't see this reconciliation happening.

"A new commandment I give you. That you love one another."

"I do love her; I just don't like her."

"Do you think you were likable when you first met me?"

"No, I know I wasn't."

"As I have loved you, that you also love one another. By this, all will know that you are My disciples, if you have love for one another."

He had loved me when I was unlovable, and when even I didn't like myself. He had loved me sacrificially, laying down His life, paying the debt for the sin in my life. He had loved me relentlessly, throughout all those years when I never even acknowledge Him. He had protected the infant me from certain death even when He didn't know if I would ever choose to live life with Him. He saw me at my worst and chose to love me. He believed in the possibility of the me He had created.

"Oh, love like that! Sigh!" Sitting in sadness expressed through that heavy sigh, the Scripture replayed in my heart again. I said, "I can't love like that. Only You can love like that, Jesus. If you want her loved, you will have to be the one that loves her." His response came immediately and powerfully.

"I'm trying to love her through you. Will you open your heart and let me? It seems impossible to you, but with Me it is possible. Will you come with me and let me show you how?" I didn't know how this would all end, but everything in my soul wanted to take this journey with Him.

When I took the step down the path toward reconciliation, He illumined His earthly ministry. Holy God waded into teeming humanity; into the worst of situations and invited the broken, blind, lame, and diseased to come to Him. He then healed, delivered, set them free, and He set down boundaries. *"Go and sin no more,"* and other directions pointed the way for them to not return to the old ways. He never participated with them in the old ways. He always called them out, and if they chose not to follow Him, He let them sadly go away, the way the rich young ruler had. Through it all, He never stopped loving them. I knew I needed to open my heart and let Him show me how to love my mother.

He then showed things about her life I had never known. The

reconnection with her was on a different level. Within the context of her story, I began to understand her as a woman. I saw the wounds she had carried, understood the pain-driven world in which she lived. The alcohol was meant to numb the pain. As she drank, it ignited her inner fury caused by the unfairness of what had been done to her. The fury always masked the pain, and it never brought a cleansing, healing fire to her soul.

The Great Depression in America referred to the poverty which had arisen from a severe nationwide depressed economy. But it became the root of a greater depression in the souls of those who lived through it. My mother's parents forced her to marry at sixteen years of age because they were so poor they couldn't afford to provide for her. She was not able to finish school because she had no shoes to wear. The newly acquired husband was an abusive, sexually perverted man who perpetrated heinous and torturous acts on her, resulting in her inability to have children. At eighteen years of age, she left him, moved to the closest big town, took a job as a waitress, and scraped up enough money for a divorce. She worked hard, very motivated to succeed, for there was no backup plan. No one to help, nowhere to go; she alone had to provide for herself. She was promoted at the restaurant. The businessmen frequenting the lunch counter noticed her work ethic. She was soon offered a job at the local newspaper office, causing her job situation to improve significantly.

In those days, the newspaper business was dominated by pow-er-grabbing, hard-drinking, foul-talking men whose "good ole boy" system was the only way to survive. She had already had her identity as a woman wrenched from her. So she learned their system, matched their behavior, and drove herself to gain new positions and new power.

She ultimately rose to the top in the southern newspaper association. However, she was always denied access to any position other than secretary in the national group because she was a woman. This was a cruelly ironic message that she would never rise above the weakness associated with being a woman, a vulnerability that had placed her in the hands of an evil man and opened the door to her own torment. She had been abused, limited, and had every dream of rising above the damage squashed by poverty, prejudices against women, and the seeming powerlessness to change any of it. She was a woman operating out of deep wounds. Her life proved the saying that, "It is hurt people who hurt people."

God gave me a vision of what He had assigned me to do in her life. This vision came first as a dream, it came often, and it would also flash into my mind when I knew I was going to see her. In the vision, I continually rubbed "The balm of Gilead" on her, tirelessly, endlessly, lovingly; just rubbing the balm while speaking no words and never understanding why. I didn't know what the vision meant, but I drew from it the understanding that He wanted me to continue to love and lift her up, to help her heal.

Boundaries became very important to me. The only boundary I had known before this part of my journey with her was simply to leave. A wide chasm between people provides a great boundary, but it keeps people out. Healthy boundaries protected the life in me while inviting others to come close to share that life. When her rage flared and threatened to engulf me, I learned to say something like, "I love you very much, but I'm not willing to have this kind of conversation with you. When you are ready to have a respectful conversation, I hope you will call me. I'm hanging up now, but I hope we can talk again soon." The first time I said those words to her, I did so with shaking hands, weak knees, and silent tears streaming down my face. Finally, when I was able to take a deep box-breath, I felt like I could fly. Imagine pressing a helium balloon down with your hand, and then suddenly releasing it. It shoots up, reaching for the highest of highs. That is the image of a soul released from bondage. I was free from the fear of her wrath and free from the pain of the love-defeating barbs she inflicted. I was finally free to love her; just as He had loved me, I could now love her because I saw her as He saw her. She was a child He thought was worthy of dying to save.

During this part of my spiritual journey, I was reading the story of Nehemiah leading the people to rebuild the wall around Jerusalem. I gained a profound understanding when I realized the work of building this protective barrier joined the people together. They took turns moving the rocks, and they also took turns taking the position of warrior against their enemy, who tried to interrupt their progress. I began to understand that when I took offense or labeled her as hopeless, I was agreeing with the enemy who wanted to stop God's rebuilding of our relationship. Scripture from Ephesians 6:12 reminded me we aren't here to fight against flesh and blood, but we must find a way to stand against the rulers of darkness and the effect they have on our relationships. He wanted her to be reconciled to me so she could then be reconciled to Him. The phrase, "the ways of Jesus" came into my heart. All my talk about trying to follow His ways took on new meaning. He chose to die to himself to save us. I had to make the same choice. I chose to die to my right to be offended, and die to taking up an offense from things she did. I also died to the desire to be treated differently by her. The hardest death for me was letting go of what

I wanted things to be. I couldn't keep that alive and love her in the reality of what was. I stopped fighting for my rights, I stopped fighting against her, and I joined Jesus as a warrior to fight for my mom to break free from her tormentor.

He helped me establish boundaries, which prompted a change in her behavior toward me. Finally, there became a point of reconnection and then the growth of a tenuous relationship. I began to understand that although she never expressed love to me in the way I yearned to be loved, she had loved me the best way she could love from the brokenness of her own heart.

During her last five years on Earth, we had a very sweet relationship. We shared heart talks, and I told her how grateful I was for the good things she had given me; the strong work ethic, the belief you can do more than you think, the strength I learned from her. I thanked her for making sure I had good manners and used correct grammar. I thanked her for sharing her story with me. I knew it had been difficult. She had never told anyone else. She told me she admired the way I loved my children, and she said she wished we could have had a relationship like I had with my kids. I told her the revelations I had about Jesus and how much I loved Him. She offered to pay for a trip to Israel so I could learn more about Him.

Her very last words to me came in the form of a handwritten note I received four days before her death. I'm sure God prompted her to write it. In it, she wrote, "Don't ever worry about me; I'm in the Lord's hands. I'm going to be fine." The same day I got the note in the mail, I also got a call telling me she had suffered a massive stroke. I flew to her bedside, and every day I rubbed lotion on her, praying for her as I rubbed her back, her arms, and massaged her hands. She could no longer speak, but she motioned she was ready to go. When it was time, she passed calmly and gently into heaven's realm with a countenance of peace. I'm eternally grateful that God let me have that time with her. Later I came across the words to an African-American spiritual, *"There is a balm in Gilead to make the wounded whole; There is a balm in Gilead to heal the sin-sick soul."* What an incredible privilege for me to see Jesus as that balm that healed her soul.

Mother-daughter relationships are deep, spiritual connections. As I have drawn closer and closer to God, He has continued His transforming work in me. Recently, I was praying for a breakthrough in the area of being in a leadership role at church. *"Jesus, why do I resist this so much? I love to serve, but why do I always sidestep being in a church position of leadership?"* In response, I got a vision of my mom. He showed me that my image of women in leadership was tied to becoming "manly." Other women in leadership who became rather harsh and dictatorial reinforced that view. In a church conference, a woman pastor taught that if you want to serve in leadership, lose the ruffles and lace! As I came into deep prayer with Him, He told me He had crowned me with loving-kindness, and I needed nothing else but to be the woman He made me to be; complete with ruffles and lace.

Deep prayer and reflection on the role of women in the church brought other insight into my response to leadership roles. Jesus' earthly ministry was developed and grown by women who supported Him. Many of the early churches experienced a significant impact because of the women leading them. Jesus went out of His way to go to Samaria to meet the woman at the well many believe to be Photina. Most Jews would not have gone the way He went, yet His word says, "But He needed to go through Samaria." Jesus spoke in public to women frequently, something that was not done, and here He speaks to a Samaritan woman which was really never done. Not only did He speak to her, but He also talked about Scripture with her! I believe He knew the impact He would have on her. When she tasted His living water, she went back into town and spread the good news. There are reports she became a leader in the development of the Christian faith. Eastern Church leaders declared Photina equal to the Apostles. Ironically, she was later martyred by being thrown down a dry well. After His resurrection, His first command to go and spread the good news was to Mary, a woman. Phoebe, Junia, Lydia, and other women named in Scripture were instrumental in the leadership roles of the first, emerging church. All are beautiful examples of Jesus calling women into leadership in His church.

Freedom work to bring healing to past hurts has several areas of focus. The area which has the most significant impact on hurting hearts is work done on parent wounds. The second-largest area is hurts inflicted by religion. Citing instruction from Paul's writings, many pastors claim they are adhering to New Testament instruction when it comes to not allowing women to hold leadership roles. Yet, they include women when they take a count of how big their membership is, something that was not done in New Testament days as illustrated in the headcount as Jesus fed bread and fish to the multitudes. Scripture taken in context is used by Holy Spirit to show the timeless heart of God revealed in ancient times. It is an error to pick which parts to bring into today and which part to proclaim as bound in the distant past. God's universal church is filled with those He inhabits and raises up to lead. The day is coming when as we worship together, we will do it in Spirit and see the Truth of who He has called to lead us. Then will end the religious wounding in the hearts of the women Jesus loves and calls into leadership in His ministry.

Through the years, I frequently said my mother's life was lived as a needless casualty of the unhealed effects of sin. But no more. That day, as I let my deep prayer time about leadership continue, He showed me how my mom now looks in heaven. I saw her completely joy-filled, laughing, and radiating love. She is now entirely who He created her to be for eternity, and she has realized her true worth as His child.

Father Wounds

After I married and left my parents' home, several things changed. My mother hired another maid to keep the house. She bought a dishwasher. And my father transferred from the job in the other city and returned home.

I never said a word to him about what I felt when he left. I never felt anything about him returning as soon as I left home. It was a closed matter. I understood. I had been lucky that he had done so much for me. I was lucky he had spent all that time with me. I was unlovable, and he had finally realized it. It was fine. I was over the pain. I was so over the pain that his name did not appear anywhere on my Master List.

It was years after making the list before the Lord asked me about him. I was in the kitchen, putting the finishing touches on his birthday cake. He liked spice cake with pecans on top. As I completed the array of pecans spreading out from the center of the cake, I heard the question, *"Why are you making that cake?"* I knew it was the Lord because we spoke often. My answer was simply, *"To take to my father for his birthday tomorrow."* The question and answer dialogue continued, *"Why that particular cake? "Because it is his favorite." "How do you know?" "He told me, and he says mine is the best one he has ever eaten." "Do you believe him?"*

This stopped me for a bit. I knew this was going to continue, and it wasn't just about a cake. I put the cake in the cake carrier, washed up things in the kitchen, and retreated to my prayer chair to begin this work He wanted me to do, but now, I had some questions to ask Him.

Jesus was magnificent in the unfolding of the journey I had with my father. There had been no "luck" nor coincidence involved. He had been chosen as the one to come and save my life because of his goodness, his gentleness, and his faithfulness. He was a powerful counter-balance to the evil of the other men who had been in my life and to the onslaught of angry attacks in our home. As I pressed in to see my father the way Jesus saw him, I kept hearing, "Man of his word." I knew this was very true. Anything my father said he would do, or even said he might do, he did. He walked in the integrity of his word. He had been a dedicated employee for over thirty years for a company always in a state of flux, who often changed everything about the way they operated. My father never complained; he carried out his duties and honored the company.

He, too, had been raised during the depression. His parents worked hard to survive, and his father was forced to take a job requiring much travel. My father was the oldest of three boys whose mother suffered from debilitating asthma. This required him to grow up rapidly, assume responsibility, and help take care of his family. It was a very different time in America. As a young boy, he rode his bicycle to school with his rifle strapped to the handlebars. After school, he went to the woods near his home to shoot rabbits, birds, or squirrels so the family could have meat to eat at supper that night.

After my grandmother passed away, my father gave me her diary. It was amazing. It was written over five years and contained only facts, dates, and details of their lives. There were no expressions of emotion, neither good nor bad. My grandmother referred to the woman who had been her closest friend for many years as "Mrs. Pitton" in her private diary. Emotions were not discussed. That spoke volumes to me. People overwhelmed by their situations have no energy for the emotions; the unspoken rule is to focus on survival, leave the feelings alone.

I began to understand why my father believed having a child would cure my mother's anger. But one day, as I was thinking about my father leaving as soon as I learned to drive, the Lord brought a dream to help me see him in a different way. In the dream, my father's clothes and body were shredded. It looked as if a large lion had clawed him until his skin was in small pieces hanging loosely all over his body. I kept trying to help him, but I couldn't. Blood was everywhere. He was getting desperate and kept saying, *"We have to do something fast. We have to get out of here."*

I awoke in tears. Surprised, I understood he had not been leaving me at all. Al-Anon taught me that part of the cycle of addiction and co-dependency is the "Let's try this next" mentality. A child didn't help, but now he thought since she was so mad when she got home from work, perhaps a "geographical cure" would force the job out of her life, and she would stop being angry so much. But she refused to participate in the move. I now understand her job satisfied her deep-seated need to be validated.

My next question was, *"Why did he stay married to her?"* Scripture after Scripture became highlighted for me. Moses, in Deuteronomy 23, teaches, *"If you make a vow to the Lord your God, don't avoid keeping it. The Lord, your God, expects you to keep it. You would be guilty of a sin if you didn't."* My Father would never break a vow, particularly one he made in a holy matrimony setting. I read the story of Jacob and Leah. Jacob did not get the wife he had been promised, yet he honored his marriage vow and kept his word. And then, I was shocked by a warning that brought so much insight to me as I read Proverbs 20:25. *"It is a trap to dedicate something rashly and only later to consider one's vows."* My parents married seventeen days after they met. Caught in the trap of a rash decision made at the height of World War II, he never wavered or backed off of his vow before God. And because my precious Savior had me come to Him with all of this, admit the truth of the pain, and surrender it to Him, He showed me my dad had never wavered in his loyalty to me either.

My dad lived for fifteen years after my mother had gone to heaven. He never once spoke any words against her. He never became bitter about all the chaos and anger and pain he had endured. We had many adventures together and many days to just enjoy each other in peace and in the ordinary things of life. I was very grateful for those times. Occasionally I have felt sad that it was never different for him in their marriage. It is a well-known saying that *"The saddest things in life are not what was, but what might have been."* I thought about how things had changed between my mother and myself, as God helped me respond differently to her. If my dad had gone to Al-Anon, would he have been able to change things? I knew the deep emotional work would have been very hard for him. I understood she had rarely been open to listening to what others had to say because of her own defenses. Her pain was too immense for her to address. My moment of regret for him in his journey was changed as God showed me my dad had found favor from God by being chosen to marry my mother. God, our heavenly father doesn't want anyone lost, and I can see that of all the good men there are in the world, He assigned my dad to the mission of loving my mother with a steadfast love because He knew Dad would honor God in that journey. This same character quality my dad had was why God knew he could entrust a ragged, bruised, broken-hearted little girl to him as well.

First breaths and last breaths are where we often experience the Presence of God most intently. At age ninety-two, when my father drew near to his entry into heaven, we had our last conversation shortly before he took his final breath. "Dad, is there anything you want?" I asked. His answer has stayed in my heart, and I know it was a gift from God. "There is nothing in this world I want, and nothing in this world that I need," came his reply spoken with all the gentleness I knew to be him. I had a deep sense this statement had been true for him for his whole life. He had enjoyed, appreciated, and experienced so much of the world during his life, but his need, his desires were not bound to the earthly. He reached out, took my hand in both of his big powerful ones, looked deep into my eyes, and said, *"I love you, Babe."* Those words came from deep within him and removed any lingering doubt I may have had.

Sovereign God delivered a sweet treasured gift to me when he gave me into the care of this man. I know as he moved into the heavenly realm, he heard, *"Well done, good and faithful servant; you have been faithful over a few things, I will make you ruler over many things. Enter into the joy of your lord."* It will be so exciting for me to see all God has made him ruler over in His kingdom and to meet him again and witness his joy.

CHAPTER EIGHTEEN

Humility

WHEN WE ARE HEALED OF DEEP SOUL WOUNDS, GOD ENTRUSTS others into our care and gives us the opportunity to share what He has done in our lives to offer them comfort and encouragement. That began to happen in my life. There were so many mother wounds, and father wounds impacting the women on my life's path. To lovingly be able to encourage them in their healing became a way for me to gain purpose in my life. Unfortunately, I lost my footing when I began to take ownership of this new opportunity.

"I never hear from God anymore!" I whined. "Well, tell me what you asked to hear from Him," replied the woman who had been walking with me for a while. God had sent an army of strong women to intersect my path at different times during my spiritual journey, and she was the strongest yet. They all had different names and wore different labels; mentor, sponsor, counselor, pastor, but they all had the same assignment from Him. To intersect me where I was and help me come up a little higher and experience Him more fully.

As our walk continued that day, I explained that after all, I had been serving God very faithfully. I completed my defense with plenty of examples of all I had been doing. Then I strengthened my case with the accolades others had shared because it was so apparent I was putting so much good out there. And yet, God was not speaking to me about a difficult situation. My exhaustive rant finally was allowed to wind down, bringing in its wake what soon became an uncomfortable silence. A few steps later, we came to a bench, where she firmly invited me to have a seat so we could take a look at this. This woman often led me in a quiet, directed prayer time seeking God. Just as I relaxed in comfortable eyes-closed anticipation of a sweet encounter, she instructed me to ask God to show me where I was still in bondage to sin. My eyes flew open! I sat straight up, and I retorted with strength so as to straighten out this misunderstanding, "I am not in bondage to any sin anymore!" Her only response was to slowly stand with gentle movement and step away from me a couple of steps. Looking me over from head to toe, she remarked, "Hmmm. Well, I didn't think you had turned to white light yet, and since you haven't, there is probably some sin still lurking in you somewhere. If you do sincerely want to hear from Him, perhaps we can take a look and see." In her gentle way, she reminded me there is only one who is perfect, and when we begin to believe we are perfectly free from sin and elevated in our righteousness, we have just stepped over into pride. She invited me to spend time in the Bible, looking at what Jesus taught about pride. The following weeks of prayer and study became a crucial time producing a profoundly spiritual work establishing a very solid step on His pathway.

She had me start with the last time I knew I had heard from Him. It took a bit of work for me to get honest with myself about that. It clearly was when He had prompted me to once again reach out to a woman I had decided was never going to turn around. She and I had a long history of her taking a step forward and then ten steps backward. In our spiritual work together, she would get right up to the point of breakthrough and then balk. She had worn me out. So, I chose to ignore His prompting. Like Jonah with Nineveh, I was ready to walk away, harboring a hardness in my heart about her. I had taken ownership of getting her redeemed. In her resistance to redemption, I had gone over to the other side, literally agreeing with the enemy of her soul when I pronounced she was a hopeless case. The root of it was my pride. I wanted to be her way to salvation, and she was obviously not cooperating.

Deep, Godly sorrow overtook me. How could I, of all people, become like that? I spent time in confession and repentance with Him. As I studied Scripture, I got in touch with Jesus' heart when He addressed sin. He was by far harsher on pride among the religious leaders than He was on any other sin. He had to be. I began to understand that when I took ownership of any work in His kingdom, I was asking Him to please step down off His throne because I could now take it from here. I had made an idol out of the spiritual gifts and talents and wisdom He had given me and elevated them as mine; I had replaced Spiritual guidance and wisdom with my own agenda.

Jesus' first instruction to His disciples in His Sermon on the Mount was to be poor in spirit. I realized it is first because He can use us only as far as our humility will allow us to go. He paid a very high price to come and pay for my sins and to lift me up and into His kingdom, and it is only when I continually empty out my self-centered spirit and let Him fill me that I can be blessed by His Presence and used by Him to bless others.

It is, after all, His Kingdom. It is not a democracy where we get a vote and get to choose what it is we want. We are all too flawed and too shallow and self-centered for that. He knows the end from the beginning. He knows eternity; we can barely know what will happen for the rest of this day. He knows what each of us truly needs. Left to my own rule, "I want what I want," and seldom is it what I need. I want easy; He wants eternal. I want pleasurable fun; He wants productive fruit. I want momentary happiness; He wants to make my joy complete. He is Holy; my soul longs to be.

He has created every human being. He knows each of them from before they were formed; He knows the number of their days; He knows the plans and purposes He has for them. I simply do not have enough information in the natural realm to know any of that for any of them. My only hope is to ask Him to show me what He wants me to know about them, what He wants me to say to them, and to put a guard over my mouth, so I don't go forward without Him. Some situations call for me to be anointed with boldness to speak the truth about what they are doing. He alone imparts that boldness. He will not give words unless they come from a heart which believes in the power He wants to give each person. His power enables them to live in a better joy-filled way.

And it is His great and eternal Church where His Spirit carries out His ministry. Whenever I say "I" led someone to salvation, brought a redeeming message, restored someone, etc. it is a red flag that I have stepped over onto an unlit step. "I" can't do any of that; only He can. Anytime one of His children humbles themselves and lets Him heal them, He gets them ready to bless others with the heart message He has given them. It was inspiring to remember what a blessing that is.

2 Corinthians 1:20-22 is a moving reminder for me. *"Jesus has always been and always will be for us a resounding "YES!" For all of God's promises find their "yes" of fulfillment in him. And as his "yes" and our "amen" ascend to God, we bring him glory! Now, it is God himself who has anointed us. And he is constantly strengthening both you and us in union with Christ. He knows we are His since He has also stamped His seal of love over our hearts and has given us the Holy Spirit like an engagement ring is given to a bride; a down payment of the blessings to come!"*

That is enough. That is abundantly, exceedingly more than enough!

CHAPTER NINETEEN

Free In Deeds

As I hear the first notes from Tchaikovsky's *"The Waltz of the Flowers,"* my soul stirs, and in my mind, I begin the dance. I know it by heart, and in my mind's eye, I see myself wearing the same beautiful costume with the long ballerina skirt, which sways in perfect response to my movements. I once again feel the strength of my body, and the fullness of transcendent joy and freedom produced as well-practiced, disciplined movement expresses deep emotion by joining with sounds and rhythm. It's my dance, my first solo, my forever dance, choreographed years ago by Miss Adrianna for me to dance. It was beautiful and perfect. The dance she had given me served me well in the spring recital. The response of the audience and my fellow dancers was wonderful and satisfying. My life's journey required me to learn new dances, ones better suited for future times and different music, but I always treasured the joy I experienced while dancing this one.

Sitting in the audience in a performance hall surrounded by others who were enjoying the Christmas tradition of *The Nutcracker* but lost in my own reverie of the dance, Holy Spirit whispered to me, *"It's time to learn a new dance."* I had no idea what that meant, but I was anxious to explore what He had to show me.

I was still in the process of "emptying out the carafe," and I knew this was part of that process. It was not about ballet; it was about the dance I did in the world with other people. Instead of pirouettes, He began to reveal the repeating cycles of behavior I had learned under the hands of another taskmaster. He began to speak to me about the strongholds stored deeply in me just as solidly as the steps, rhythms, and movement of the dance. As always, He did it gently, gradually, and from a beginning point of revelation rather than recrimination.

Just like my response to the first notes of the music from *"Waltz of the Flowers,"* I quickly and instinctively responded to other people when I found myself in a situation similar to previous encounters. A stronghold is a heart-held belief system built over time based on our experiences in the world. This system is a web of lies, inner vows, and self-protectionism that is contrary to the way God wants our lives to be lived. The depth and breadth of the works of darkness had laid out a vast area of work to be done in this part of my redemption. He had me reread the Master List. There had been considerable progress in His work to show me the truth of who I was, and now, He began to show me the work I needed to do with the ones who had hurt me. He began to help me understand that from the actions of one man, I had come to believe lies about all men. From the actions of one person in authority over me, I believed lies about all authority figures. Because of one group of girls, I generalized lies about all girls, and so on and so on and so on. The list was long, and the work was deep.

The mechanics were simple. When something painful occurred in my life, I drew a conclusion about that event. Then I formed something I believed to be rational truth from what happened. Based on that rational truth, I sought ways to protect myself from having to experience that pain ever again.

This rationalization process is not always a negative thing. If I lift a lid off the pot on the stove and the knob on the top burns my fingers, I form and store the truth, that pot lid gets hot. The next time I use that pot, I protect myself by using a potholder to lift the lid. This is a good use of information about something in my life. But, when I get a new set of pots that have knobs that stay cool, I have to decide if they are like the old lids, or not. Usually, I will withhold my trust in the new lids until I have thoroughly tested them because of my experience with the old lids. Similarly, when a close friend betrayed me, I believed I could not trust other women. To protect myself, I stayed shallow in friendships. My shallowness acted like the "potholder;" it protected me from being hurt.

While those mechanics sound simple, working through relationship strongholds is not as simple. To continue to do the same old things always gets the same old results. As Jesus was addressing this issue in John 8, He states, *"If the Son makes you free, you shall be free indeed."* As I read it through again, I read it as "in deed." If I let Him set me free, then I am free in my deeds, free to do things differently. I am no longer bound to my old patterns, yet they cling to me, and it takes Holy Spirit to help me break their dominance.

One of my underlying beliefs was that if I let people get close to me, they would reject me. This lie was deeply rooted and reinforced by my belief that I was unlovable. Even as my journey of love with Jesus began to break off the first lie, the lie I believed about others was unmoved. I had special filters highlighting rejections. So at the first sign of rejection, I responded by withdrawing to protect myself. I stayed distant and shallow in relationships and would walk away from the other person if there was any indication they might reject me. It was double-walled insulation. If I stay shallow, then I don't let you know the real me. That way, you will only be rejecting who you think I am, not me. I also won't let you in very far because you have to be expendable in my life so I can walk away to protect myself. The bereft and lonely world runs on this fortified stronghold. Living life dominated by strongholds results in continual chaos, sadness, and hopelessness. If my protective withdrawal pattern comes into play with a person whose self-protection is through angry outbursts, it triggers in me another deep stronghold of detachment, so I don't have to face the anger. Through these protective actions, we each set up another hurtful event. In this way, we fortify the learned lie into a stronger "truth" in the depth of our soul. The downward spiral continues in an ever-deepening pit of distrust and joyless living.

Scripture repeatedly tells us God wants to be our God, wants us to be His children, and He wants to live among us; all of us and bring unity. Working from the Master List on the lies I believed about others began to bring healing and compassion in new ways within my soul. This is not a matter of a procedure or steps to take. It was inviting Holy Spirit to come and work within me, cleaning out the mire, bringing God's light, and then letting me see others in the light of His love. Over time I took each person on my list into my deep prayer time. I asked Him to speak to me about that person, and about that situation. I asked for His truth and wrote out every Scripture He gave me. Then I confessed all the hurt I had caused others because of my protectionism. Seeking repentance, I asked Him to show me how He wanted to be my protector.

Knowing my repeating patterns and learning how to do it differently within relationships with others are two very different things. The brain forms deep patterns that affect our responses in ways we often don't realize. Many of my patterns were formed in early childhood in situations that were no longer in my conscious mind. My heart had not forgotten, and just as surely as my early formation determined the shape of my nose, my patterns were shaped by my early relationships and the trauma they brought.

God brought a wonderful man into my life. He is gentle and kind; he genuinely loves me. The first time we met, God gave me a vision of how He saw Stan. He's a big man who walks in authority, a mighty man, a man of confidence, a man's man, a leader. Yet, I saw him as a little boy, and God whispered to me that if I would love him, he had a great love to give me. We got to know each other over time and married. We are very different. One day I asked Stan if I ever did anything which was outside his comfort zone. Laughing, he replied, being married to me was outside his comfort zone. And yet, he delights in me and I in him.

We laugh frequently, we walk through hard times holding on tightly to God and each other, we encourage each other to be all God wants us to be, and we go on grand adventures together, knowing Who leads the way. As my husband, he is my defender and is steadfast in doing his part to see that my life is good and very safe. And yet after twenty-six years, at this writing, living day-in-day-out with this good man, there are times when I react out of stored patterns. The simplest example I can relate is how I responded to an ordinary question he once asked, "Hey, where is my blue shirt?" This was during the first year of our marriage. I had gotten out of the shower and was drying my hair while singing along with Sandi Patty and Larnelle Harris, who, from my cassette player, proclaimed the Lord is *"More Than Wonderful."*

In my full abandon of myself to the worship of my Lord, above the noisy task of hair drying, I was unaware of anything around me. My husband spoke this innocent question with the volume needed to break through to me amid the noise of hairdryer and song. In a moment of unbidden, deep visceral response, I squatted in the fetal position and covered my head. At first, he thought I was joking, but when I turned off the hairdryer and looked up, he saw the tears in my eyes. He held me tightly while I recovered and listened intently as I explained that loud voices trigger a response in me going back for years.

That day, and for every day since, anytime my husband approaches a room where he knows I am busy and possibly unaware of his approach, he whistles. He whistles a little tune to let me know he's coming my way. He whistles a little tune to let me know I'm safe. He whistles a little tune to let me know he cares. He whistles a little tune to say he loves me. Over time the trigger has diminished. I rarely have a negative response, but still, my husband whistles.

Vicious cycles that continually cause pain and chaos stem from strongholds of trauma, lies, and self-defense, which result in other people responding negatively. That brings about yet another trauma producing an ever-strengthened vicious cycle. A popular sixty's song was the theme song from the play *Carnival*, *"Love Makes the World Go Round."* That is a wonderful sentiment, but in the lives of wounded people, strongholds drive the cyclical activity of their world.

The reference in 2 Corinthians verse 10 to strongholds carries with it a definition as well as a way to bring them down. *"For though we walk in the flesh, we do not war according to the flesh. For the weapons of our warfare are not carnal but mighty in God for pulling down strongholds, casting down arguments and every high thing that exalts itself against the knowledge of God, bringing every thought into captivity to the obedience of Christ, and being ready to punish all disobedience when your obedience is fulfilled."*

A stronghold is every argument raised against the knowledge of God and His ways. Lies about my identity, other people, and about the nature and character of God are strongholds. Those lies lived in my mind, were felt in my emotions, and had strengthened my will to protect myself so I could defend my lies. My self-protectionism had distanced me from others, from God and even from coming to know myself. Stuck in that state, I elicited negative responses from others, proving my lies were true.

In the example with my whistling husband, the lie I believed was that people raising their voice meant they were angry, and they would hurt me. Had someone I wasn't married to raised their voice at me I would have left in order to protect myself. In the safety of my marriage, I could be honest about what I was feeling; but first, I had to decide to believe what Christ had shown me. I had to decide that Jesus was with me, and He would keep me safe; that freed me to love my husband and give him a chance to love me even with my weaknesses.

Choosing to interrupt the cycle and to hold my thoughts in obedience to Christ changed everything. It brought down that stronghold. And Stan's ongoing whistling changed a wrong pattern of thought which I had clung to for years. I do matter, and I can do things differently. Doing things differently opens the way for relationships to grow and become better.

This is not a task which any of us can carry out with sheer force with gritting teeth and by faking it until we can finally make it through another painful encounter. It began for me with the decision to be willing to do His will. Like the woman caught in adultery, I was grateful for the freedom His salvation had brought me, and I deeply desired to be able to *"Go and sin no more."* I had been beaten up and trampled down by sin. Not just what had been done to me but also what had been done by me. I knew there was more to life than what I had known. I had met a living, vibrant Savior who had saved me out of darkness, and now I wanted nothing else to do with darkness. I was highly motivated to follow His ways.

Jesus studied the Torah, treasured the teachings from His ancestors, and committed Himself to follow God's ways recorded in the scrolls. Many times as I read the Old Testament, I read it aloud. It was the way Jesus had studied it so much of His time on earth. There is a place in my soul that stirs up when I read from Deuteronomy, particularly in the sermon Moses gave on the Mount long before Jesus delivered His.

"I call heaven and earth as witnesses today against you, that I have set before you life and death, blessing and cursing; therefore choose life, that both you and your descendants may live; that you may love the Lord your God, that you may obey His voice, and that you may cling to Him, for

He is your life and the length of your days; and that you may dwell in the land which the Lord swore to your fathers, to Abraham, Isaac, and Jacob, to give them."

When I want to retreat into my old, awful-yet-comfortable ways, I hear these words. It awakens my will, and I choose differently. I choose life for my family and myself, and I cling to Him and His ways leading to Life. Why would I choose otherwise?

CHAPTER TWENTY

Warfare

"FOR THOUGH WE WALK IN THE FLESH, WE DO NOT WAR ACCORDING TO THE flesh." Many churches do not teach about warfare. I was oblivious for years about anything having to do with demons or the dark world of Satan. I read this scripture in 2 Corinthians:10, yet didn't completely understand what it was saying. But I began to notice things that were supernatural in nature and began to ask God to teach me. It was amazing how many teachings He prepared for me, how He cleared my schedule so I could sit at the feet of teachers and pastors teaching on the subject, and how He began to highlight Scripture to show me what He wanted me to know. As I studied, listened, and read books, it seemed that many people live their life believing there is a demon behind every turn of life, lurking in the parking lot, and ready to interrupt believers' lives at any second. Yet, that seemed contrary to life living in the kingdom of God.

After a year of these weighty teachings, one day, I just became overwhelmed with it all and cried out for Him to give me the "bottom line" on what He wanted me to know. Two days later, I found myself sitting in a movie theater as probably the oldest person at "The Avengers." In a scene that took on enormous meaning for me, Loki, the evil god who was trying to take over the earth, is prancing around yelling at the Hulk, "I am a god you dull creature, and you will not bully me!" Hulk then grabs Loki, pounds him onto the ground, and then throws him with enough force to break through the concrete. With a disdainful look at the battered Loki, Hulk storms away, and glancing over his shoulder declares Loki is a "puny god." Holy Spirit whispered to me, "*That is what I want you to know.*" There is an enemy who is all puffed up and trying to take over, but he has no claim on believers. The One who saved us is far more powerful than he is; indeed, he is a puny god compared to the One True God.

I came to new awareness through a Bible study, which has helped me understand why we still have the deeds of darkness around us. When Jesus rose from the grave He won the battle against Satan. He went to hell and took away the keys to show He had control over it. He told Peter the gates of hell would never prevail against His church. That was an important illustration. The city gate in Biblical times was where all business was handled, where plans were made, contracts agreed upon, and where rulers met with their leaders. Jesus overcame all the plans and plots and power of Satan. When He said the gates of hell would not stand, he was saying the plans would not stand, and the contractual agreements made with Satan would be broken. We currently live in the middle ground of a Kingdom that is both seen and unseen. It is here now, and it is still coming to be completely fulfilled. Jesus has defeated Satan, yet the final round will not be fought until Jesus comes again. In the meantime, it became essential for me to understand the working of the enemy so I could avoid him.

My work led me to Scripture in Ezekiel 28 and to Isaiah 14, where there is a description of Satan's heart. *Your heart became proud on account of your beauty, and you corrupted your wisdom because of your splendor. You said in your heart, "I will ascend to the heavens; I will raise my throne above the stars of God; I will sit enthroned on the mount of assembly, on the utmost heights of Mount Zaphon. I will ascend above the tops of the clouds; I will make myself like the Most High.*

From this teaching, I began to understand how a small opening a believer gives to the works of Satan can become a big deal. The enemy of our soul is never satisfied until he is elevated above our Lord. A little bit of our life means nothing to Satan; he wants dominance and rule over everything. If I tell a little lie of convenience, that is not a terrible sin, and there is grace and mercy for me to repent and receive forgiveness; however, it opens up space in my soul for a lying spirit to enter. A successful simple lie opens the way for dishonesty to enter into other areas of life. Holy Spirit living in me is never comfortable with lying. John 16 tells us when He, the Spirit of Truth, has come; He will guide us into all truth. Scripture distinctly names fourteen demons, and for each one, there is also Scripture that helps believers overcome the working of them. The only way a believer can become influenced by them is to open a door that allows spiritual darkness to enter into their life.

The very nature of the devil is deceitful, and he is a master of disguising our sins so that we don't even see them. However, God has been so good to provide Scriptures that we can all use to help us examine our life. Proverbs 6:16-19 is very straightforward and has helped me see error in my life. *"There are six things that the Lord hates, seven that are an abomination to Him: arrogant eyes, a lying tongue, and hands that shed innocent blood, a heart that devises wicked plans, feet that hurry to run to evil, a lying witness who testifies falsely, and one who sows discord in a family."* As I continued to look for the ways of Jesus, I found Paul's letter of instruction to the Ephesians very helpful for staying on the Lighted path. In 5:1-13, *"Be imitators of God, as dearly loved children. And walk in love, as the Messiah also loved us and gave Himself for us, a sacrificial and fragrant offering to God. But sexual immorality and any impurity or greed should not even be heard of among you. Coarse and foolish talking or crude joking are not suitable, but rather giving thanks. Know and recognize this: Every sexually immoral or impure or greedy person, who is an idolater, does not have an inheritance in the kingdom of the Messiah and of God. Let no one deceive you with empty arguments, for God's wrath is coming on the disobedient because of these things. Therefore, do not become their partners. You were once darkness, but now you are Light in the Lord. Walk as children of Light for the fruit of the light results in all goodness, righteousness, and truth discerning what is pleasing to the Lord.*

As I delved deeper into my study and asked Jesus to help me prepare to live a life of spiritual warfare, He led me to Ephesians 6 and a new spiritual discipline of armor-wearing. It began one morning after my prayer time with Him as I was preparing to dress for the day. I was excited because I had a new outfit and I was meeting friends for lunch. As I took out my new clothes and their accessories, I said aloud to myself, "I'm so excited to wear this, it's so cute!" And He asked, *"What are you going to do before you put on those clothes?"* I waited for a second and wondered if I was missing something—after all, mine was a rather obvious answer. *"I'm going to brush my teeth and take a shower."* His response came quickly, *"That's a very good practice."* I didn't hear anything else and went about my day. I was engaged in an ongoing Bible study and the next morning, I found the text for that day was Ephesians 6. The big, bold heading was "The Whole Armor of God." He spoke into my spirit, *"That's what I want you to practice wearing every day."* I spent several weeks journaling about that chapter, and by the end of that time, He had given me a spiritual discipline. It is still part of my heart work I often do; it has become a "very good practice" for me. This is the way He led me to wear His armor each day.

Verse 10 - 13 *"Finally, my brethren, be strong in the Lord and in the power of His might. Put on the whole armor of God that you may be able to stand against the wiles of the devil. Therefore take up the whole armor of God that you may be able to withstand in the evil day, and having done all, to stand."*

My work took the following form as I responded to each line of Scripture, sought God's input and His words about sin in my life. Then I confessed, repented, asked for His Forgiveness and Strength:

"Stand therefore, having girded your waist with truth,"

My Response: "Holy Spirit, will you show me any lies I believe about You, myself, or about others?"

"having put on the breastplate of righteousness,"

My Response: "Jesus, I know your work on the cross is the only righteousness I can claim, but I want to walk like you. Will you show me any areas of my life where I am not walking in your ways? Will you strengthen me so I can walk the way you would have me walk?"

"and having shod your feet with the preparation of the gospel of

peace;"

My Response: "Holy Spirit, will you show me any place where I am not at peace? What is the root of the unrest? What do you want to say to me about that? Will you help me share the gospel Truth with those around me?"

"above all, taking the shield of faith with which you will be able to quench all the fiery darts of the wicked one."

My Response: "Holy Spirit, will you show me any place in my life where I have more faith in what I see than I have in Your Truth? I repent from that. Will You give me your Truth in this? I choose to believe it!"

"And take the helmet of salvation."

My Response: "Jesus, thank you for paying such a great price for my salvation. Will you show me any disobedient thoughts I have? I choose to believe in Your Truth in every situation."

"and the sword of the Spirit, which is the word of God;"

My Response: "Holy Spirit, will you give me a greater understanding of God's word and teach me how to live by these Holy Teachings?"

"praying always with all prayer and supplication in the Spirit, being watchful to this end with all perseverance and supplication for all the saints."

My Response: Prayer for all the wonderful servants of the Lord surrounding me in my life and serving the kingdom throughout the world.

We will have tribulation and attacks from the enemy of our soul. We can't wait until the battle comes to try to find our armor. We must be prepared. This simple exercise has given me a focus to keep the door shut to any works of the enemy of my soul. It began as a morning-time exercise, and I often worked through it as I prepared to start my day. Just as my morning shower cleansed my physical body, this cleansed my soul.

One morning I was reading the story of David coming to face Goliath, I thought of the armor of God practice. David refused the battle armor offered him by Saul. I thought of all the times in my life I had tried worldly answers for my problems. They never "fit," nor produced good results. David knew his battle wasn't against flesh, so he wouldn't battle in a worldly way. He had on the spiritual armor God had given him. I could see evidence of it. David was facing a giant of a problem that appeared to be totally impossible to solve, yet he knew the Truth of the power and presence of God, so he never wavered. He took down that giant, impacting the lives of his family and his community. Now, when I feel a spiritual attack stirring around me, I smile and say what David said to his enemy, Goliath, "*Who do you think you are to defy the armies of the living God?*" but I always add, "*You puny god!*"

CHAPTER TWENTY-ONE

Forgiveness

THE LAST PIECE OF MUCK AND MIRE STORED IN MY HEART WAS another obstacle to the fullness of walking on His path with Him. It was big and deeply entrenched. He had been gentle and kind and let me cling to it until it was time to let it go.

To know Jesus is to know forgiveness; it is the gift He gives to each of us as He comes and invites us into His kingdom to live with Him. Forgiveness is an often-taught topic from the pulpit. It was something I had given voice to many times. But even when I was parroting Jesus' words, *"Father, forgive them for they know not what they do,"* deep in my soul, I harbored hidden thoughts. *"Yes, they did too know what they were doing. I did not deserve what happened to me. I was the one left to walk in despair. I lived covered in shame that they should wear. They don't seem to have suffered any consequences from their actions."* These and other obviously "un-Christian" thoughts ran through my soul.

Every time I heard a sermon teaching that forgiveness is a decision, one which we must make because Jesus chose to forgive us, I would tighten my resolve. My oft-repeated litany, "I will forgive them, I will forgive them," took on the cadence and pace of "the little train that could" phrase, "I think I can, I think I can." I would then shush the cry for justice that kept springing up in my heart, at least for a while.

I just couldn't rectify the idea that I had been the victim, and any court of law in America would mete out punishment to those who had hurt me. Yet here in Christiandom, I felt guilty for thinking those thoughts. I felt too much shame even to admit what happened to anyone in the church. Jesus said, *"For if you forgive men their trespasses, your heavenly Father will also forgive you. But if you do not forgive men their trespasses, neither will your Father forgive your trespasses."* He said it right there at the end of the model prayer He taught us to pray. Right there early in His ministry in Matthew 6! My breakthrough came when I could longer manage the tension between what I kept hearing from the pulpit, reading from my Savior's words, and the cry for justice that kept echoing in my soul. I wasn't searching to be right, but oh, how I needed to understand. I needed to know if He had cared about what they did to me.

Studying the entire Bible, not just the New Testament, I realized I had compartmentalized Jesus. After all, He brought us the New Covenant, so He had been my focus. But it was only through inviting Holy Spirit to reveal more of who God is through the continued study of His Word that I began to understand Jesus' teachings with a new depth of understanding. When people would say, "Jesus was a Jew," early in my faith, I would always respond, "Well, His mom was Jewish, but I think His Father is non-denominational." In my ignorance, I minimized the importance of Jesus' in-depth study of God's Word in the Torah. He quoted Deuteronomy each time Satan tempted Him in the wilderness. He read from Isaiah to proclaim the mission of His ministry. His first ministry pronouncement to people was to say, "Repent" and come back to the covenant God made with Abraham. It was when I embraced the entirety of the Bible, understanding the role of the Israelites and the Jewish teachings that I began to understand the fullness of Jesus' teachings. My journey into understanding forgiveness began in Genesis.

We know the story of Adam and Eve. Eve yielded to the temptation to try to take the place of God and invited Adam to join her. By partaking of the fruit of the tree of knowledge of good and evil, they revealed they wanted to rule their world based on what they thought was the good thing to do. One only has to take a brief look around us today to see that same attitude prevalent in our world and to notice the mess it has made of our lives. God sent them out of the garden so they wouldn't live forever in their fallen state of delusion about their own goodness. They must once again come to know their great need for Him to rule in their life. Just before He sent them out, He took off the fig leaves which they had decided were a good thing to wear, and He clothed them in animal skins.

As I considered that, the importance of that act became clear. God had given Adam the task of naming all the animals. Naming is important to God, and this was a significant job. As Adam came to know and understand each animal, he would give them an appropriate name. Standing at the point of eviction from paradise, Adam and Eve would have clearly and deeply understood the cost of their sin. The skins God gave them that day were taken from the very animals they had tended. They felt the wages of their sin as they put on the skins. God was illustrating the death that sin brings. Hopes, dreams, relationships, opportunities, and life itself dies when sin is allowed to rule in our lives. He requires the sinner to make an act of sacrifice to acknowledge the gravity of their actions.

The Bible records stories of mankind and their continued journey away from God; then, with their confession, repentance, and sacrifice, they return to Him. Throughout the Old Testament, the ancient men acknowledged that all sin is against God. His ways are the ones we are breaking. With the coming of our Savior, animal sacrifices are no longer required. However, when we focus only on mercy and grace, we tend to overlook the teachings about confession and repentance. We lose sight, miss the pain, and don't consider the excruciating cost of the sacrifice He made for us.

Jesus said, *"If you are bringing your sacrifice and remember that your brother has something against you, leave your sacrifice there, go and be reconciled to your brother, then come and offer your gift."* Each morning, as I bring my life to Jesus, He wants me to consider the state of the life that He has given me. How have I handled the precious things from heaven He has placed in my life? What He treasures most are people, and when He places someone in my life, I know He is entrusting the care of that person to me. When I thoughtlessly, carelessly hurt someone, Holy Spirit prompts sorrow in my heart. Sincere Godly sorrow causes tender pain in my heart. I hurt when I have hurt you. Here in His teaching, Jesus commands us to go to the person, confess that we know we did wrong, offer acts of repentance, and ask for their forgiveness so we can be reconciled.

He further instructed us to go to someone who has hurt us and tell them how we feel. He gives great detail in Matthew 18 about going alone and if the person who hurt us doesn't listen to go back and take some witnesses. This teaching was so hard for the deeply-entrenched desire in me to avoid all conflict. The Scripture was clear after all efforts have been made; the goal is to confront the person with their need to repent and to be willing to offer God's forgiving love when they do. Through this, I finally grew in my ability to find my voice and speak up when people hurt me. Usually, in the very act of communication, a new and higher understanding was gained for us both; and the relationship was strengthened. We get to know people more intimately when we can be honest and forthright and seek to understand. God's ways always surpass the results we expect.

Sinners were and still are called to repent, to go confess to those they have harmed, and to make restitution when they should and can. There is mercy and grace offered to those who do this. To admit our sin and to ask for forgiveness from those we have harmed is an important step, a step that builds relationships and allows us back into close communion with God. It is the way we can walk with Him in His kingdom now. We honor Him when we honor those He put in our lives. In the teaching that we must forgive to be forgiven, Jesus is instructing Christians. We must be ready to offer forgiveness to those who have sinned against us when they come in repentance and humbly ask. That is how God forgives us when we come, confess, and repent when we accept Jesus as our Savior. It is what He does when we confess our failings daily, change the way we live, and seek Him.

My problem as I studied through the Scriptures was that no one from my dark past ever came asking me to forgive them. That was the key to forgiveness. Jesus paid the price for all sin, but His forgiveness is given to those who come, confess, repent, and then gratefully receive it. Yet, I knew He wasn't telling me to hold on to the unforgiveness in me and the bitterness it had brought into my heart.

What I honestly wanted was justice. I wanted them to suffer because they made me suffer. I wanted to hold court; I could testify endlessly about the depth of the abuse, the betrayal, public shame and humiliation, the physical pain, ridicule, the demeaning way I was treated. I could also judge them. They were horribly wrong to mistreat an innocent. Going through my list, I could find every one of them guilty. And I could sentence them. They had no right to live their life as if I had never mattered, to never acknowledge the pain they had caused; they had to be held accountable. In the moments spent getting honest about what was in my heart, Jesus was right there with me. He knew, He understood, and He asked me to transfer all of that out of my heart by giving it to Him. *"Vengeance is Mine."* He said; I nodded. *"Forgiveness is Mine to give."* "Yes!" I agreed. *"Redemption is my heartbeat."* That caused me to pause. Jonah wouldn't go to Nineveh because he knew if he told them about God, they would turn to Him and be redeemed. I understood how Jonah felt. I prayed hard about that. God wanted not one to be lost. My Mother wounded people her whole life because of her unhealed wounds. I knew I had hurt other people because of the hurt done to me. Perhaps all those from the darkness who hurt me had done what they did because of what people had done to them. Could that be what was behind their action? If I took them out of the courtroom in my heart and gave them over to God's courtroom, what would happen? Could I release them to God knowing He would save them if at all possible? Realization came and brought Light; if He saved them, they would be changed. None of us can meet Him and not be changed. With Him in their heart, they would feel sorry for what they had done. They would know I mattered. There would be justice. Finally, slowly, thoughtfully, my response came. "So be it, I will let this be finished by You Lord."

I lifted each one along with the cloying darkness still living in my heart and gave them to Him. True worship and adoration for Him flowed out of me that day more than ever before. He had taken the darkest part of the mire out of my heart. As He did this, He respected and honored me; He never minimized any of it. He had hurt when I was hurt, and letting me know He hadn't forgotten about any of it, He also let me know He genuinely cared. He is a just and holy God who reassures me, instills me with security, and restores my hope.

Released from the heavy burden of judging and punishing others, I began to see people differently. It is sometimes a difficult task to see the truth of who people are in Christ because it is hard to see beyond what they are doing. There is no redemption offered as long as we either condemn them by labeling them as their sin or believe that what they are doing is the limiting fact of who they truly are.

Thinking back to the story in John 8, the scribes and the Pharisees bring a woman to Jesus. He is told she was a woman *"Caught in the act of adultery"* it was enlightening to me to see she is not labeled "Adulteress." Adultery was something she publicly did. But Scripture is clear; it is not who she was. Jesus tells her to go and sin no more. That is one of the most empowering statements in Scripture. He believed in her—He believed she could be all He created her to be. He doesn't condemn her because of her mistake, and He believes in the truth of who she truly is now that she has met Him. He believed she would rise above what she had done to be who He created her to be. He had that same faith and hope in me. He has it for all people.

Jesus' words further reveal His heart in Luke 5 when he says to the paralyzed man lowered down through the roof, *"I say to you, arise, take up your bed, and go to your house."* He explained that it was the faith of the man's diligent friends which had brought about the healing. Jesus didn't accept the state of the man's body as the truth of who that man was. I knew He was teaching me to see beyond the actions and limitations of the people in my life and to have faith in who they are after they encounter and embrace the risen Savior.

There is an old legend about how the first diamond was found. My sweet husband, Stan, told me the story as he presented an exquisite diamond ring to me. The folklore says that as miners dug deep inside a mine shaft, they uncovered a rock which seemed to shine with a light through a crack in its outer crust. As they peeled away layer after layer of mud and dirt, the brilliance of the stone shone forth. According to this legend, the name given to this stone was "dia" "mond," meaning "Stone of God" because they believed it had God's Light inside. When my husband gave the diamond to me, he said, "I wanted to give you a stone which had as much of God's Light in it as you have in you, but this was as close as I could get." While God was redeeming the broken pieces of me, He brought this precious man into my life who now saw God's light in me. Little did I know I would come to understand my husband was speaking words to me which aligned with how God saw me.

Later, Jesus gave me a compelling vision. He had me go back and see myself as a child again. I saw the dirty, scarred child in my memory. He immediately said, *"That is not you."* Confused at first, I almost stopped. "If that isn't me, then who is it?" I asked. His answer was gentle, *"That is who you have come to believe you are. You let the things done to you and the things you did because of it define you. But that is not you. I made you and nothing that has been done to you or by you can ever change who I made you to be."* As His soothing words washed over me, the image I was experiencing began to change. I saw a clean, happy child with golden curls. Then watched in amazement as from within her, a brilliant glow began and burst forth in light beams shaped in many facets. Then in a breath-taking array, I watched as other brilliant, beautiful light-filled beings came to join me. *"My greatest treasure, My most beautiful creation, is everlasting and lives within each of my children."* Peace flooded my soul as joy swelled in my spirit.

Revelation came in waves. I now understood the first dream of seeing other people on the path. It was not a specific group of people who lived a certain way or joined a particular denomination He wanted me to find. He returned me to my original state of being that He had created. As He did, I have encountered others who are living that experience. In the presence of these "people of Light," there is a glorious sense of God that is greater than I have ever experienced alone. When He freed me from relationship strongholds, I became able to connect at a heart and soul level with others. My journey would never have been as joyous and exciting had I not been able to connect with His other children. He created us to be together, and there is so much more to life when we are in unity as a family. We are walking in the eternal kingdom revealed only in part now, one which will be beyond our imagination when we experience its fullness. My true identity was never hurt or damaged by my journey here on earth. Just like that diamond buried deep in the earthly mire and darkness, I had not become the darkness. I have always been and will always be a creation of the Light. I am who He made me to be; I always was, and I found "me" when I met Him. I didn't realize the fullness of my identity until He gave birth to the Light in me. The power of the Light showed me the face of Jesus, and in it, I saw my reflection.

CHAPTER TWENTY-TWO

Postlude

THE DESIRE TO BE OUTSIDE PUSHED ME BEYOND MY AVERSION TO the cooler fall air. I found my usual place atop the low stone wall running along the back of my yard. I settled myself on the stones that had absorbed every ray of sunlight and graciously shared their warmth with me. At first, I basked in the feel of the sunlight on my body as it radiated energy into me. Enjoying the warming from the stones, I closed my eyes. Connecting to that sense of peace found in His creation, all the clamor of the world fell away. Opening my eyes again, I stared into the clear sky noticing the cobalt blue was intensifying, indicating the summer sky was giving way to fall. Change is our ever-present state. I remembered back to when I first sat on this wall.

Just beyond the wall was a grove of giant live oak trees. When I first came, they were a safe haven for squirrels and birds to settle down, feed, and raise their young. Life was abundant and joy-filled in the oak neighborhood. The squirrels were the clowns, often running along the wall, then bursting into near flight as they jumped into the shelter of the canopy of leaves. The birds filled the air with song. Listening as they called to one another, I often imagined conversations they were having. *"Look at me, look at me, look at me!"* was often a phrase from the male mockingbirds wanting to carry out the plan to keep the species alive. They sang incessantly when the eggs hatched and loudly reported the event to the world. The redbirds sang their songs to their little nesting ones encouraging them to learn the ancient call passed down through the ages. The twittering chirping from the nervous little wrens and sparrows tugged at my heart when they sang louder than they seemed large enough to do. The drumming of the woodpecker always added the timpani and cadence. The white-winged doves brought a smile to my face when they gave voice to a sound similar to a chicken with a sore throat. A deep stirring in my soul connected and moved with the mourning dove calls. What delight I shared with God out on my wall as I imagined He was enjoying the ever-present sounds and activity of life He had made.

During another time of contemplation on the wall, I noticed something which changed everything. That day I felt, rather than saw, a large bird fly swiftly over my head and land in the nearest oak tree. Intrigued, I watched as the sleek bird launched from the branch to resume his journey. *Wow, I've never seen a bird so powerful or athletic.* It seemed to fly with no effort, no flapping, and with an intensity that startled me. For days the air over the trees seemed to be filled with these birds as they effortlessly circled and soared so high I had to squint to see them. Drawn in by their ability, I went on a quest to identify them. Eventually, with help from my daughter, I found out they are called "kites." It seemed to be a cute sounding name for a bird that indeed hung in the sky, using only the currents to move it along. But it was soon apparent there was nothing cute about this bird. Powerful, intent on only their needs, they came to be a menace to the sanctuary of the oak tree neighborhood. Once, I watched as one circled twice from high above the trees, and finding his target, dove from sky to tree with bullet-like accuracy, and never slowing his pace grabbed a baby mockingbird from the nest. Day after day, they took anything they wanted from nests, from the ground, from the canopy of the trees. Day after day, the joyful explosion of sounds decreased, and ultimately, the music of the birds stopped. I decided to rename the kite. To me, they will always be the *"joy robbers."*

Sitting on my now-silent wall, I felt *"smad,"- so sad I'm mad!* The activity in those trees mirrors the effects I see in the world around me. I've seen countless lives being lived out in happiness, and contentment suddenly changed when that foreboding dark presence moves in. *"In this life, you will have tribulation,"* we are told. Yet, when it comes, we let it overtake us; we give it all the power. We stop living our authentic lives, shrink into our fears, and continue as scared shadows of what we were meant to be. We seem to forget we can have peace in our Savior. He says to us, *"Take heart! I have overcome the world."*

As I reflected on this, I heard a kindred soul crying *coo-ah, coo, coo, coo.* My heart answer came, *"Yes, precious dove, I too will keep singing the song He has put into my heart."* The testimony of this lone, brave little bird doing what God created her to do even in the darkest day re-centered me. There is still much work He has prepared for me, and I won't let the residual darkness left in the world rob me of the joy that is abundantly mine through His salvation! I am walking around every day with the most costly, most luxurious gift the world has ever been given living in me. He put it there so I could take it to the hurting people He brings into my life. How could I ever keep quiet about that?

I sat on the wall remembering the Light-led path I have walked. With each step, I have gotten closer to God. He has lovingly revealed His nature and character to me during the journey of my life. He has gently, patiently mended my soul. He has also given me all the precious things of heaven. A little while back on a summer day, I was enjoying being with my family for a cookout. The sunlight sparkled in the summer breeze, my children and friends were laughing and talking; the grandchildren were running around, filling the air with their joy when Holy Spirit pulled me into a frozen-in-time moment. He whispered, *"I planned this day for you long ago; I knew you would seek Me, and I wanted to fill your life with moments like this."* I remembered the long-ago accusation I flung at Him, *"All I have ever asked you for was a happy family; is that too much for you?"* He had given me exceedingly, abundantly more than I could have ever imagined. Our family has our tribulations and challenges, but He is with us all helping us to overcome. Within our family I find my "no matter what" place; no matter what we will love each other and be there to support one another.

He has also extended my "family." I have had incredible spiritual mothers who encouraged me, loved me, and called me to come up higher. Spiritual fathers, walking with peace and power of Spirit, have shared their testimonies inspiring me to want to continue to draw closer to God. Their testimonies aren't the story of how they came to faith thirty years ago; they are about recent, relevant experiences with their living, present Savior. I have new spiritual sons and daughters who found me because they were drawn to the Light they could see in me, and oh, how they wanted more of that. And now, He is bringing spiritual grandchildren seeking words of wisdom; they are craving more of the Light as they go into this ever-darkening world with a fresh passion for glorifying their Father.

This journey back through the darkness with all its muck and mire reminds me of what I have been saved *from*. Through the years, He graciously has shown me what I was saved *for*. Only He could have given me the passion for reaching out to a world hurting from the effects of abuse and anger to bring them the message only He could have given me. He has allowed me to witness the tremendous power His Light brings into people's hearts as they encountered Him. I've had fantastic opportunities to watch as He returns people to the way He created them to be as His Light clears away the mire in their soul. I've been privileged to see their countenance change as they begin to reflect Him. I've gotten to hear their stories, told in breathless wonder, of how their lives have changed.

With each step, I have also gotten closer to the time when my instruction and revelation here on Earth will come to an end. There in the sunshine, I closed my eyes, envisioning that time. My pathway leads me to the very top of the solid rock where He gave me life. Light swirls around me, my arms reach as high as possible as I, on tiptoe, sway and ready myself for Him to come and draw me into the rhythmic dance of True Life. I am singing the song of Praise He taught me to sing using all the fullness of the last glorious breath He gives me, and then I dance into His welcoming arms!

And now may, "The grace of our Lord Jesus Christ be with you all. Amen."

ABOUT THE AUTHOR

Peggy Corvin, Freedom Minister, Speaker, Teacher, and Trainer lives outside Nashville, TN and shares the joys of life with her husband Stan, their kids, and grandkids. She is passionate about being a bold Truth teller who calls others onto the Lighted path of God. She particularly loves helping other women find their silenced voices and tell of their journeys out of darkness into God's Light.

"Getting to sit across from other children of God as they come into His presence and experience freedom is the most wonderful of all the gifts He has ever given me; It is watching the miracle of Life grow in another person!"

Made in the USA
Columbia, SC
27 August 2020

18229286R00093